KT-553-712

contents

Now that you're a fully fledged student and embracing independence, you're going to want to know how to cook up a storm in the kitchen. *The Student Cookbook* is here to allay any fears you might have about making your own dinner, and if you're already a budding cook, to give you some fresh inspiration. All the recipes are easy and delicious! Some are super-quick, while others need time in the oven or on the hob to work their magic. Either way, they are stress-free and designed to satisfy, whether you're coming home late with a mammoth hunger after a big night out, or you're having friends over for a lazy Sunday lunch. Make sure you check out the tips in the following pages before you get started – they will make life a whole lot easier and ensure that your culinary efforts are always successful, undaunting, and above all, fun.

introduction

kitchen know-how

The recipes in this book need the minimum of kitchen equipment. Some recipes, like the desserts, will require extras, e.g. a handheld electric whisk (which can be bought very cheaply), a baking tin for brownies, etc. but you can go a long way with these essentials:

2 or 3 sharp knives, including a serrated knife

wooden spoon

fish/egg slice

potato masher

garlic crusher

pepper mill

tin opener

vegetable peeler

cheese grater

2 chopping boards
(1 for meat and 1 for veg)

large mixing bowl

sieve

colander

1 large and 1 medium saucepan

frying pan with a lid

baking tray

roasting tin

ovenproof dish (Pyrex or ceramic)

measuring jug

weighing scales

a selection of airtight containers

kettle

toaster

aluminium foil

clingfilm

greaseproof paper

kitchen paper

cleaning stuff, including washing up liquid, sponges and surface cleaner

tea towels

oven gloves

Every recipe has at least two of these symbols:

 serves 4 — This tells you roughly how many people the recipe should serve

 Q — This is an extra-quick recipe, and shouldn't take you longer than 20 minutes once you've prepared the ingredients.

 V — This is suitable for vegetarians, but that's not to say that meat-eaters won't enjoy it too!

 M — This recipe includes some meat or poultry.

F — This recipe includes some fish or seafood.

Additionally, where a recipe calls for salt and black pepper, use sea salt and freshly ground black pepper if at all possible. They give the best flavour.

Whenever a recipe calls for olive oil, if you are using it raw (e.g. in a salad dressing or drizzled over vegetables), the extra virgin variety is the tastiest. For frying or roasting, use a basic (not extra virgin), mild variety.

handy ingredients

sea salt	*risotto rice*	*tomato purée*
black peppercorns	*dried pasta, including spaghetti*	*a selection of dried herbs, such as oregano*
olive oil	*couscous*	*a selection of dried spices, such as curry powder, ground cumin, paprika, chilli powder or dried red chilli flakes*
vegetable or sunflower oil	*stock cubes or bouillon powder*	
balsamic vinegar	*tinned chopped tomatoes*	
red or white wine vinegar		*Marmite*
dark or light soy sauce	*a selection of tinned beans, such as cannellini, kidney*	*honey*
tomato ketchup (as if you needed reminding!)	*tinned tuna*	*butter or margarine*
mustard	*plain flour*	*milk*
mayonnaise	*sugar*	*onions*
long grain rice		*garlic*

food safety

• Always keep your kitchen clean! Keep it tidy and disinfect worktops after use with a mild detergent or an antibacterial cleaner. Keep pets off surfaces and, as far as possible, keep them out of the kitchen.

• Store food safely to avoid cross-contamination. Keep food in clean, dry, airtight containers, always store raw and cooked foods separately and wash utensils (and your hands) between preparing raw and cooked foods. Never put cooked food on a surface that you have used to prepare raw meat, fish or poultry without thoroughly washing and drying the surface first.

• Wash your hands with hot, soapy water before and after handling food, and after you have handled raw meat and fish.

• Never put hot food into a fridge, as this will increase the internal temperature to an unsafe level. Cool leftover food quickly to room temperature, ideally by transferring it to a cold dish, then refrigerate. Cool large dishes such as stews by putting the dish in a sink of cold water. Stir occasionally (change the water often to keep the temperature low), then refrigerate once cool. During cooling, cover the food loosely with clingfilm to protect it from contamination.

• Don't use perishable food beyond the 'use-by' date as it could be a health risk. If you have any doubts about the food, discard it.

• Reheated food must be piping hot throughout before consumption. Never reheat any type of food more than once.

• Frozen meat and poultry should be thoroughly defrosted before you cook them otherwise the centre may not be cooked, which could be dangerous.

• If you are going to freeze food, freeze food that is in prime condition, on the day of purchase, or as soon as a dish is made and cooled. Freeze it quickly and in small quantities, if possible. Label and date food and keep a good rotation of stock in the freezer.

• Always leave a gap in the container when freezing liquids, so that there is enough room for the liquid to expand as it freezes.

• Always let food cool before freezing it. Warm or hot food will increase the internal temperature of the freezer and may cause other foods to begin to defrost and spoil.

• Use proper oven gloves to remove hot dishes from the oven – don't just use a tea towel because you risk burning yourself. Tea towels are also a breeding ground for germs so only use them for drying, and wash them often.

- Hard cheeses such as Cheddar, Gruyère and Parmesan will keep for up to 3 weeks if stored correctly. Once opened, fresh, soft cheeses such as cream cheese should be consumed within 3 days.
- Leftover tinned foods should be transferred to an airtight container, kept in the fridge and eaten within 2 days. Once tins are opened, the contents should be treated as fresh food. This doesn't apply to food sold in tubs with resealable lids, such as cocoa powder.
- The natural oils in chillies may cause irritation to your skin and eyes. When preparing them, wear disposable gloves or pull a small polythene bag over each hand, secured with an elastic band around the wrist, to create a glove.
- If your kitchen is prone to over-heating, it is best to store eggs in their box in the fridge. Keep them pointed-end downwards and away from strong-smelling foods, as they can absorb odours. Always use by the 'best-before' date.
- Wash hands before and after handling eggs, and discard any cracked and/or dirty eggs.
- Cooked rice is a potential source of food poisoning. Cool leftovers quickly (ideally within an hour), then store in an airtight container in the fridge and use within 24 hours. Always reheat cooked cold rice until piping hot.

ingredients tips

- When substituting dried herbs for fresh, use roughly half the quantity the recipe calls for, as dried herbs have a more concentrated flavour.
- Chop leftover fresh herbs, spoon them into an ice-cube tray, top each portion with a little water and freeze. Once solid, put the cubes in a freezer bag. Seal, label and return to the freezer. Add the frozen herb cubes to soups, casseroles and sauces as needed.
- The colour of a fresh chilli is no indication of how hot it will be. Generally speaking, the smaller and thinner the chilli, the hotter it will be.
- To reduce the heat of a fresh chilli, cut it in half lengthways, then scrape out and discard the seeds and membranes (or core). See also 'food safety' above for advice on handling chillies.
- Most vegetables keep best in the fridge, but a cool, dark place is also good if you lack fridge space. Potatoes should always be stored in the dark, otherwise they go green or sprout, making them inedible.
- To skin tomatoes, score a cross in the base of each one using a sharp knife. Put them in a heatproof bowl, cover with boiling water, leave for about 30 seconds, then transfer them to a bowl of cold water. When cool enough to handle, drain and peel off the skins with a knife.

- To clean leeks, trim them, then slit them lengthways about a third of the way through. Open the leaves a little and wash away any dirt from between the layers under cold running water.
- Store flour in its original sealed packaging or in an airtight container in a cool, dry, airy place. Ideally, buy and store small quantities at a time, to help avoid infestation of psocids (very small, barely visible, grey-brown insects), which may appear even in the cleanest of homes. If you do find these small insects in your flour, dispose of it immediately and wash and dry the container thoroughly. Never mix new flour with old.
- If you run out of self-raising flour, sift together 2 teaspoons of baking powder with every 225 g plain flour. This will not be quite as effective but it is a good emergency substitute.
- Store raw meat and fish on the bottom shelf in the fridge to prevent it dripping onto anything below.
- Store coffee (beans and ground) in the fridge or freezer, or it will go stale very quickly.
- Store oils, well sealed, in a cool, dark, dry place, away from direct sunlight. They can be kept in the fridge (though this is not necessary), but oils such as olive oil tend to solidify and go cloudy in the fridge. If this happens, bring the oil back to room temperature before use.

• To de-vein large prawns, cut along the back of each shell using a sharp knife and lift or scrape out the dark vein. Alternatively, use a skewer to pierce the flesh at the head end of the prawn, just below the vein, then use the skewer to gently remove the vein.

• Small pasta tubes and twists such as penne and fusilli are good for chunky vegetable sauces and some meat- and cream-based sauces. Larger tubes such as rigatoni are ideal for meat sauces. Smooth, creamy, butter- or olive oil-based sauces and meat sauces are ideal for long strands such as spaghetti (so the sauce can cling to the pasta).

• Dried pasta has a long shelf life and should be stored in its unopened packet or in an airtight container in a cool, dry place. Leftover cooked pasta should be kept in a sealed container in the fridge and used within 2 days. Ordinary cooked pasta does not freeze well on its own, but it freezes successfully in dishes such as lasagne and cannelloni. Allow 85–115 g dried pasta per person.

• Pasta must be cooked in a large volume of salted, boiling water. Keep the water at a rolling boil throughout cooking. Once you have added the pasta to the boiling water, give it a stir, then cover the pan to help the water return to the boil as quickly as possible. Remove the lid once the water has started boiling again (to prevent the water boiling over), and stir occasionally. Check the manufacturer's instructions for cooking times. When it is ready, cooked pasta should be al dente – tender but with a slight resistance.

• As an accompaniment, allow 55–85 g uncooked rice per person or for a main like risotto, up to 115 g.

• Rice may be rinsed before cooking to remove tiny pieces of grit or excess starch. Most packaged rice is checked and clean, however, so rinsing it is unnecessary and will wash away nutrients. Risotto rice is not washed before use, but basmati rice usually is – rinse it under cold water until the water runs clear.

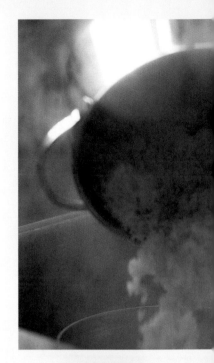

taste tips

• Try mixing a pinch or two of ground spices such as curry powder, chilli powder or turmeric with breadcrumbs or flour, and use to coat foods before frying. Add ground spices such as cinnamon, mixed spice or ginger to fruit crumble toppings. A pinch or two of ground nutmeg will perk up mashed potatoes, cheese sauce, cooked spinach, bread sauce and rice puddings.

• Stir wholegrain mustard into mashed potatoes or mayonnaise before serving to add extra flavour. Mustard also enhances salad dressings and sauces. A pinch of mustard powder added to cheese dishes will enhance the flavour.

• If you add too much salt to a soup or casserole, add one or two peeled and cubed potatoes to soak up the salt, cooking until tender. Discard the potatoes before serving.

• An excellent way of thickening soups is to stir in a little oatmeal. It adds flavour and richness too. A small amount of instant mashed potato stirred in at the last minute is also a good way of thickening soup.

• Add a little pearl barley to soups and stews – it will add flavour and texture and have a thickening effect.

• A teaspoon or two of pesto sauce stirred into each portion of a hot vegetable soup just before serving will liven it up.

• For a tasty and creamy salad dressing, mash some blue cheese and stir it into mayonnaise, or a mixture of mayonnaise and natural Greek yoghurt.

• Add some health and a satisfying crunch to salads by tossing in a handful or two of lightly toasted seeds or chopped nuts just before serving. Good ideas include sunflower, sesame or pumpkin seeds and hazelnuts, walnuts, pecan nuts or pistachios. Toasted seeds can also be sprinkled over cooked vegetables.

• If you over-cook an omelette, leave it to cool and use it as a sandwich filling. Chop the omelette and combine it with mayonnaise and snipped chives, if you like.

• Bulk out a pasta or rice salad by adding a tin of drained and rinsed beans such as chickpeas, red kidney beans or black-eye beans.

• For an extra-crunchy crumble topping, replace 25 g of the flour with the same weight of chopped nuts, rolled oats or oatmeal, or replace caster sugar with granulated or demerara sugar.

kitchen wisdom

• To remove odours from a container that you want to use again, fill the container with hot water, then stir in 1 tablespoon baking powder. Leave it to stand overnight, then wash, rinse well and dry before use.

• If you transfer foods from packets to storage containers, sellotape the food label onto the container so you can easily identify its contents and you have a record of the manufacturer's cooking instructions, if necessary. Make a note of the 'best-before' or 'use-by' date on the container, too.

• For convenient single servings, freeze portions of home-made soup in large, thick paper cups or small individual containers. Remove them from the freezer as required, defrost and reheat the soup thoroughly before serving.

• To make salad dressings or vinaigrettes, put all the ingredients in a clean screw-top jar, seal and shake well. Alternatively, put the ingredients straight into the salad bowl and whisk together well, before adding the salad.

• Spirits with an alcohol content of 35% or over can be kept in the freezer – this is ideal for those which should be served ice-cold.

• To remove fishy odours after preparing fish, rub the cut surface of a lemon over your hands, the knife and chopping board. Rubbing your hands with vinegar or salt, then rinsing and washing them, will also help to get rid of unpleasant fishy smells.

microwave safety

• The more food you are cooking, and the colder it is, the longer it will take to cook in a microwave.

• When microwaving items such as sausages or bacon that may spit during cooking, cover them loosely with kitchen paper, to avoid too much splattering.

• Many foods need to be covered during microwaving. Use microwave-safe clingfilm, a plate or a lid. Pierce clingfilm, or leave a gap at one side if using a plate or lid, to allow excess steam to escape.

• Never operate a microwave when it is empty, as the microwaves will bounce back to and damage the oven components.

• Be careful when stirring heated liquids in a container in the microwave, as they can bubble up without warning.

• After food has been removed from the microwave, it will continue to cook due to the residual heat within the food, so adhere to standing times when they are given in recipes.

• Use a microwave with a built-in turntable if possible, and make sure that you turn or stir the food several

times during cooking to ensure even cooking throughout. The food towards the outer edges usually cooks first.

• Metal containers, china with a metallic trim, foil or crystal glass (which contains lead) should not be used in a microwave. Metal reflects microwaves and may damage the oven components. Microwave-safe plastic containers, ovenproof glass and ceramic dishes are all suitable, as is most household glazed china. Paper plates and kitchen paper can be used to reheat food for short periods. Roasting bags (pierced) may be used in a microwave.

snacks and sides

guacamole

Guacamole is so easy to make and very versatile. Scoop it up with the Tortilla Chips below, use it as a dip for sticks of raw veg, spread it on toast, or have it with the Beef Fajitas on page 183 or the Chilli Chicken Enchiladas on page 78.

Using a small, sharp knife, cut the avocado in half all around from top to bottom. Twist the fruit gently and pull the two halves away from each other. Using a teaspoon, scoop out the flesh from each half into a small bowl, and throw away the stone and the skin. Gently mash the flesh with a fork to make a lumpy purée.

Stir in the diced tomato, 2 teaspoons of the lime juice and the garlic. Season with salt and pepper. Mix all the ingredients together with the fork – the mixture should be a bit lumpy. Taste and add more lime juice or salt and pepper as needed. Eat immediately before it turns brown.

serves
2–4

Q

V

1 large, very ripe avocado

1 large or 2 small tomatoes, diced

juice of 1 lime

1 small garlic clove, crushed

a big pinch of salt

a big pinch of black pepper

home-baked *tortilla* chips

Turn ready-made soft wheat tortillas into a crunchy snack by baking them in the oven.

Preheat the oven to 170°C (325°F) Gas 3.

Using kitchen scissors, cut each tortilla into 8 wedges. Spread the wedges in one layer, not overlapping, on the baking tray.

Bake them in the preheated oven for 15 minutes until they turn crisp and dry. Eat while still warm or leave to cool first.

serves
4–6

Q

V

4 large or 6 medium wheat flour tortillas

a large baking tray

½ a cucumber, deseeded
and grated

2 teaspoons salt

1 garlic clove, crushed
(optional)

150 ml Greek yoghurt

juice of ½ a lemon

tzatziki

Greek tzatziki is a versatile, low-fat dip and it also makes a
great salad dressing or accompaniment to grilled chicken and
fish or roast Mediterranean-style vegetables.

Mix the grated cucumber and salt together and leave for 10 minutes.
Put the cucumber in the centre of a clean tea towel, gather up the edges
and twist to squeeze as much moisture out as possible. Put the cucumber
in a bowl with the remaining ingredients and stir to combine. The tzatziki
will keep in the refrigerator for 3 days.

Variations:

Beetroot tzatziki Add 1 medium raw or 2 bottled beetroot, grated, and
2 tablespoons chopped chives to the mixture. This makes a great
accompaniment to boiled new potatoes.

Olive tzatziki Stir 75–100 g finely chopped stoned black or green olives
into the yoghurt and cucumber mixture.

2 tomatoes

50 g butter, softened

2 garlic cloves, crushed

2 tablespoons dried oregano

2 x 125-g naan breads

salt and black pepper

garlic and tomato naan

This recipe calls for puffy naan bread. If none is available,
you can use an Italian ciabatta loaf. Slice it in half through
the middle and spread the butter over the cut sides.

Preheat the oven to 200°C (400°F) Gas 6.

Peel the tomatoes using the instructions on page 10. Deseed the tomatoes,
remove the cores and finely chop the flesh. Leave to cool.

Put the softened butter, garlic and oregano in a bowl and mix well. Add the
chopped tomatoes and mix well to combine. Spread each naan bread with
half of the mixture. Season with salt and pepper.

Bake in the preheated oven for 10–15 minutes until hot. Cut into slices and
serve immediately.

tzatziki

cheese on toast

2 thick slices of white bread

125 g cheese, such as Brie, Cheddar or a soft creamy goats' cheese

a few drops of Worcestershire sauce (optional)

pickles, relish or chutney, to serve

serves
2

Q

V

This is one of those dishes that's perfect when you get back late from a night out – quick, delicious and washing-up-free. It tastes great with almost any pickle, chutney or relish. Two slices just won't be enough!

Preheat the grill.

Toast the bread under the grill on one side only. Slice, grate or spread your chosen cheese onto the untoasted side of the bread. Add a few splashes of Worcestershire sauce, if using, and grill for 2–3 minutes until melted and bubbling.

Serve with pickle, relish or chutney and tuck in.

cinnamon toast

2 thick slices of white bread

unsalted butter, for spreading

1½ tablespoons caster sugar

½ teaspoon ground cinnamon

serves
1–2

Q

V

The quickest treat yet invented – hot buttered toast sprinkled with cinnamon-flavoured sugar, then grilled until crunchy. Thick slices of bread, challah or brioche (two kinds of soft bread) work best, but you can also use crumpets or English muffins split in half.

Preheat the grill.

Toast the 2 slices of bread in a toaster, then spread with butter.

Mix the sugar with the cinnamon, then sprinkle it over the buttered toast to cover in an even layer.

Put the toast under the grill for 30 seconds to 1 minute until the sugar has melted and looks bubbly, then carefully remove it.

Leave to cool for a minute (the sugar is very hot and will burn your lips) before eating.

tomato, basil and
mozzarella toasts

cheese
on toast

tomato, basil and mozzarella toasts

These moreish, juicy toasts make a perfect snack or small bite
to serve with drinks. They're great just with tomatoes and basil,
but even better with a chunk of mozzarella on top.

Put the tomatoes and basil in a bowl. Spoon over the olive oil, season well
with salt and pepper and toss lightly. Set aside for about 15 minutes.

Preheat the grill.

Toast the ciabatta slices on both sides under the grill until crisp and golden.
Rub the cut side of the garlic on each piece of toast, then spoon the tomato
and basil mixture on top. Add a piece of mozzarella to each one, spoon over
the juices remaining in the bowl and sprinkle with extra oil, if using. Grind
a little more pepper on top and serve.

makes
12

V

250 g cherry tomatoes, halved

1–1½ handfuls of fresh basil
leaves, roughly torn

3 tablespoons olive oil, plus
extra for drizzling (optional)

12 slices of ciabatta, about
2 cm thick

1 garlic clove, halved

150-g ball mozzarella, torn
into bite-sized pieces

salt and black pepper

*giant prosciutto, brie
and tomato toasts*

giant *prosciutto,* *brie* and *tomato* toasts

This mammoth, melting toast is the closest thing to an instant pizza that you could wish for – with the juicy tomatoes and rocket adding a wonderful fresh zing.

Cut the tomatoes in half and put in a bowl. Sprinkle with the vinegar and olive oil, season with pepper and toss gently. Set aside.

Preheat the grill.

Set the ciabatta under the grill, cut side down. Toast until crisp and golden. Meanwhile, cut each slice of prosciutto into 3 pieces.

Turn the bread over and arrange the strips of prosciutto and slices of Brie on the uncooked side. Grill for a further 5 minutes or so until the bread is golden, the ham crisp and the cheese golden and bubbling.

Spoon the tomatoes on top, top each toast with a handful of rocket and serve immediately.

serves
2

Q

M

175 g cherry tomatoes

1 teaspoon balsamic vinegar

1 tablespoon olive oil

1 ciabatta loaf, halved horizontally

4 slices of prosciutto or thinly sliced smoked ham

175 g Brie

2 handfuls of rocket

black pepper

mushrooms on toast

Another treat that's good at any time of day, these juicy, fragrant mushrooms are really rich and garlicky. Pile them up on thick slices of hot buttered wholemeal toast or a crusty roll.

Heat the oil in a pan, add the shallots and fry gently for 2 minutes, then add the garlic and cook for a further minute.

Add the mushrooms, toss to coat in the garlicky oil, then add the white wine, thyme and a pinch of salt. Increase the heat and bring to the boil, then let bubble gently for about 10 minutes until the mushrooms are tender and the juices have been absorbed.

When the mushrooms are nearly cooked, toast the bread on both sides and spread with butter. Season the mushrooms with pepper, check if they need any more salt, then pile onto the toast.

serves
2

Q

V

1 tablespoon olive oil

2 shallots, finely sliced

1 garlic clove, crushed

150 g button mushrooms

60 ml white wine

1 sprig of fresh thyme

2 thick slices of wholemeal bread

butter, for spreading

salt and black pepper

spicy fried *potatoes* and *chorizo* on toast

3 tablespoons olive oil

200 g new potatoes, boiled and cut into bite-sized chunks

125 g raw chorizo sausage, cut into bite-sized chunks

1 garlic clove, crushed

½ teaspoon dried chilli flakes

4 slices of country-style crusty bread

salt and black pepper

This manly feast is not for the faint-hearted and is perfect when you need something quick, tasty and really filling. The crisp, golden potatoes absorb the flavours of the chorizo, and the rich, spicy, garlicky oil is just delicious when it soaks into the toast. Sprinkle with a little more chilli for extra heat.

Heat the oil in a large frying pan until hot, then add the potatoes and fry for about 5 minutes. Add the chorizo and continue frying, turning occasionally, until the potatoes are crisp and golden. Sprinkle with the garlic and chilli flakes and fry for a further 2 minutes.

Meanwhile, toast the bread in a toaster. Spoon the potato and chorizo mixture on top, drizzling over any extra oil from the pan, then serve.

pesto and *mozzarella* toastie

1 ciabatta roll, halved horizontally

1–2 teaspoons pesto

4 thin slices of mozzarella

black pepper

A variation on classic cheese on toast but with an Italian twist. This is a particularly good choice if piles of melted cheese puts that diet at risk: mozzarella is lower in fat than Cheddar.

Preheat the grill.

Lightly toast the uncut side of each half of the ciabatta roll under the grill.

Turn the ciabatta halves over and spread with the pesto. Top with the mozzarella and return it to the grill. Grill for about 3 minutes until the mozzarella melts and begins to colour. Sprinkle with a little black pepper before serving.

spicy fried potatoes
and chorizo on toast

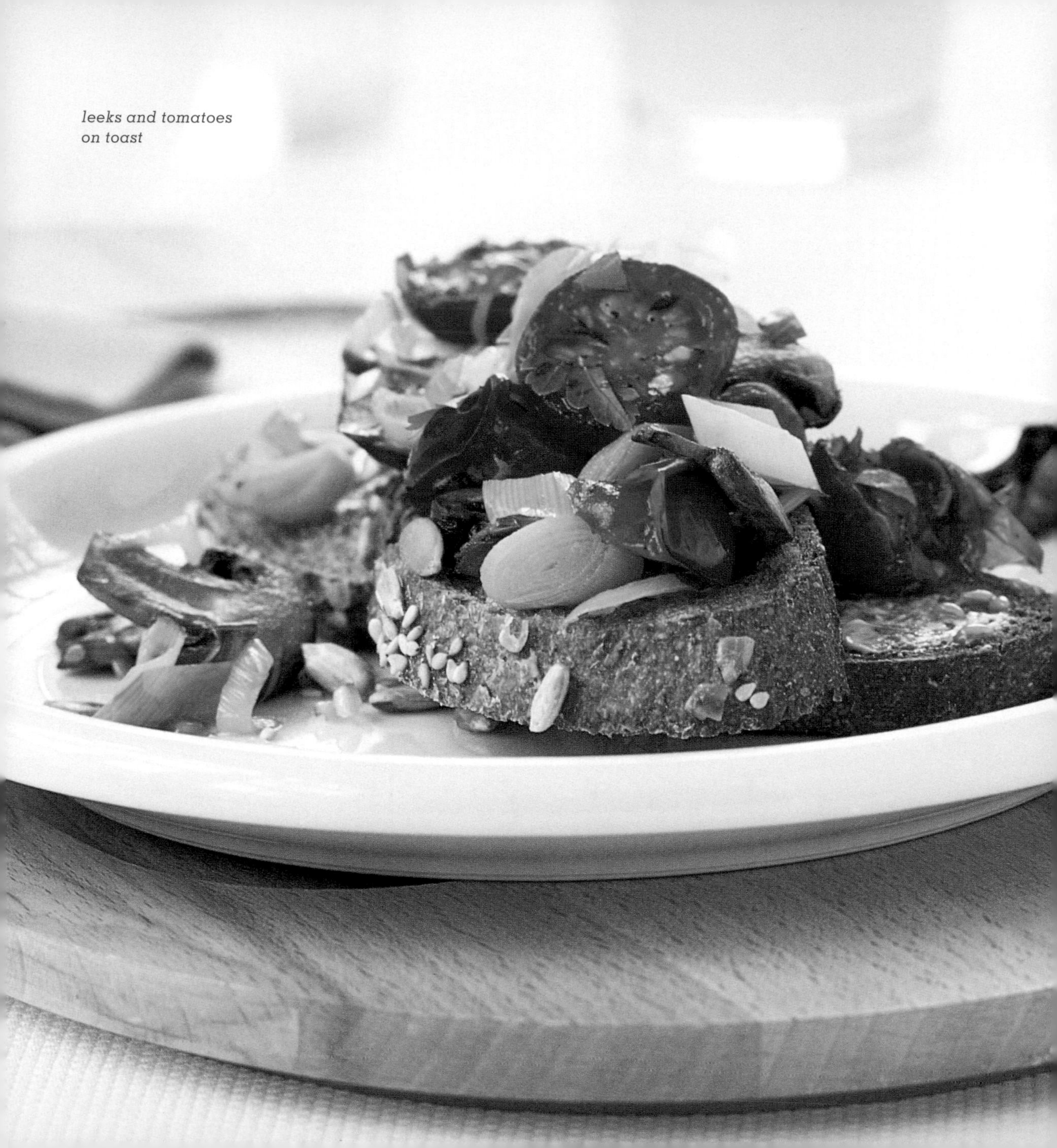

leeks and tomatoes on toast

leeks and *tomatoes* on toast

This is a really tasty suggestion for a quick breakfast, lunch or supper. Much more than just tomatoes on toast...

Heat the oil in a frying pan, add the leeks and mushrooms and cook over medium heat for 4–5 minutes, or until tender.

Meanwhile, toast the bread, then spread with butter.

Add the tomatoes and herbs to the leek mixture and cook for a further 1–2 minutes, or until heated through. Season with pepper. Serve the toast topped with the tomato and leek mixture.

Variation This would make an ideal filling for warmed split pita bread. Add 1 thinly sliced and deseeded red or yellow pepper at the same time as the leeks, if you like. If you can buy some wild mushrooms, use them instead of the button ones for extra flavour.

serves
2

Q

V

1 teaspoon olive oil

2 small leeks, thinly sliced

10 button mushrooms, about 50 g, sliced

4 slices of wholegrain bread

butter, for spreading

200 g cherry tomatoes, halved

3 teaspoons finely chopped fresh basil leaves

2 teaspoons finely chopped fresh oregano

2 teaspoons finely chopped fresh flat leaf parsley

black pepper

sardines and *tomato* on toast

Tinned sardines are an ideal storecupboard standby, and are a great source of calcium, vitamin D and long-chain omega-3 fatty acids – great brain food!

Toast the bread in a toaster, then lightly spread with mayonnaise.

Put the sardines on top of the toast, then mash slightly with a fork. Arrange the chopped tomato on top, then squeeze over a little lemon juice. Season with black pepper before serving.

serves
1

Q

F

1 slice of wholegrain bread

mayonnaise, for spreading

60 g tinned boneless, skinless sardines in olive oil, drained

1 small tomato, halved, deseeded and roughly chopped

a squeeze of lemon juice

black pepper

little fried *mozzarella* and *tomato* sandwiches

250-g ball mozzarella, torn into bite-sized pieces

16 small, thin slices of bread

3–4 tomatoes, thinly sliced

3 eggs

50 ml olive oil, to fry

salt and black pepper

serves
4

V

These are lovely because they are crisp and eggy on the outside and gooey and creamy on the inside. They are a popular snack all over Italy. Add slices of ham if you like.

Dot the mozzarella over 8 of the bread slices and lay the slices of tomato over the top. Top with the remaining bread slices and press lightly to seal.

Crack the eggs into a bowl, then beat with a fork until they are smooth. Pour them into a shallow container in which you can fit the sandwiches. Lay the sandwiches in the egg and leave them for 2–3 minutes to soak up the egg. Turn them over and leave them for another 2–3 minutes so that the other side is soaked in egg too.

Heat a little of the olive oil in a non-stick frying pan and fry the sandwiches on one side for about 3 minutes, until the bread is golden. Carefully turn the sandwiches over and fry for a further 2–3 minutes, until that side is golden too; the cheese inside should be well melted.

Cut the sandwiches in half diagonally and serve them straightaway.

garlic and *parsley* bread

2 garlic cloves, crushed

a handful of fresh flat leaf parsley, chopped

¼ teaspoon dried chilli flakes

olive oil

1 ciabatta loaf, split horizontally

salt and black pepper

serves
4

Q

V

Everyone loves this easy bread – similar to garlic bread but with a little kick from dried chilli. Eat it by itself or alongside a stew to mop up the juices left in your plate.

Preheat the grill.

Sprinkle the garlic, parsley, chilli flakes, salt and pepper evenly over the opened bread halves. Drizzle generously with olive oil, then cook under the grill until golden. Cut the bread into chunks and serve with a big bowl of pasta, such as Rigatoni with Bacon and Beans on page 73.

*little fried mozzarella
and tomato samdwiches*

gruyère, mature cheddar
and spring onion panini

french toast and fried tomatoes

Who says French toast is just for breakfast? Topping it with fried tomatoes makes a juicy, tasty snack. Frying tomatoes seems to intensify their flavour and the heat makes them soft and velvety – truly delicious on eggy bread.

serves **4**

Q

V

4 eggs

4 tablespoons milk

4 slices of bread

50 g butter

4 ripe tomatoes, halved

salt and black pepper

Beat together the eggs and milk in a large, shallow dish and add some salt and pepper. Add the bread and leave to soak for 5 minutes on each side so that all the egg mixture is absorbed.

Heat a large, non-stick frying pan over medium heat. Add the soaked bread and cook over medium-low heat for 3–4 minutes on each side.

In a separate pan, melt the butter. Add the tomatoes and fry on each side for 2 minutes, then serve on top of the hot French toast.

gruyère, mature cheddar and *spring onion* panini

This is no ordinary toasted cheese sandwich. It works best with a panini press but you can use a sandwich toaster instead. The mixture of strong cheeses with spring onion is pure heaven.

makes **2**

Q

V

4 slices of sourdough bread

50 g Gruyère, grated

50 g mature Cheddar, grated

2 spring onions, thinly sliced

salt and black pepper

vegetable oil, for brushing

Preheat a panini press or sandwich toaster. Lay the slices of bread out. Divide the cheeses between the two sandwiches, add the onions, and season with salt and pepper. Put the tops on. Brush both sides of the panini with a little oil and toast in the preheated panini press for 2–3 minutes, or according to the manufacturer's instructions. The bread should be golden brown and the filling warmed through.

Note Try this panini with a dollop of grainy mustard on the side for dipping and a baby spinach salad.

tuna melt

200 g tinned tuna, drained

3–3½ tablespoons mayonnaise

½ tablespoon capers, rinsed and finely chopped

2 small gherkins or 1 large dill pickle in sweet vinegar, diced fairly finely

¼ red pepper, diced finely

1 tablespoon chopped fresh tarragon (optional)

2 large, thick slices of white crusty bread

4 large, thin slices Swiss cheese, such as Gruyère or Emmenthal

black pepper

This is the ultimate tuna melt. Use any kind of white bread – crusty rustic sourdough, a large bloomer or a simple sandwich loaf – just make sure the slices are large and thick.

Put the tuna in a bowl and flake the flesh. Add the mayonnaise, capers, gherkins, peppers and tarragon (if using) and mix well. Season with pepper.

Preheat the grill.

Toast the bread on one side under the grill, then turn it over and spread the tuna thickly on the uncooked side. Put 2 cheese slices on top of each toast and grill for about 5 minutes until the cheese is golden and bubbling.

Note Look for tuna tinned in water rather than brine as the capers are salty enough already.

mozzarella and tuna quesadilla

olive oil, for brushing

2 large soft wheat flour tortillas

100 g tinned tuna, drained and mashed with a fork

6 slices of mozzarella, about 75 g total weight

10 fresh basil leaves

black pepper

Satisfyingly moreish, this golden tortilla parcel is filled with melted mozzarella and tuna. Diced sweet pepper, chopped spring onions, or herbs, such as chives can also be added, if liked.

Lightly brush a large non-stick frying pan with oil. Put one tortilla into the pan so it fits snugly. Spoon the tuna over the tortilla, leaving a 2-cm gap around the edge. Top the tuna with the mozzarella and basil, then season with pepper to taste.

Put the second tortilla on top of the filling, pressing it down around the edges. Put the pan over medium-low heat and cook the quesadilla for 3 minutes until the tortilla is golden and beginning to crisp.

To cook the other side of the quesadilla, put a large plate on top of the frying pan and carefully flip it over to release the quesadilla onto the plate, then slide it back into the pan. Cook the tortilla for another 3 minutes until golden and the mozzarella is melted. Slice into 6 wedges and serve.

bacon, potato and red leicester panini, with tabasco sauce

mozzarella and tuna quesadilla

bacon, potato and *red leicester*
panini, with tabasco sauce

Save your leftover baked or roasted potatoes to create this fiery, filling panini – not for the faint-hearted!

Preheat a panini press or a sandwich toaster. Cut the top and bottom off the ciabatta so that it is about 3 cm thick. Save the crusts for another use. Slice open lengthways and then cut in half.

Add a little oil to a frying pan and fry the bacon until crisp. Remove from the pan and drain on kitchen paper. Keep the pan hot, add the potato slices and season with salt and pepper. Fry on both sides until crisp around the edges. Divide the bacon and potatoes between the two sandwiches. Add a dash of Tabasco and top with the cheese. Brush both sides of the panini with a little oil and toast in the preheated panini press for 3 minutes, or according to the manufacturer's instructions. The bread should be golden brown and the filling warmed through.

makes
2

Q

M

1 ciabatta loaf

6 rashers of smoked bacon

1 large cooked potato, sliced

50 g Red Leicester or Cheddar, thinly sliced

2 teaspoons Tabasco sauce

salt and black pepper

vegetable oil, for frying and brushing

spicy
vegetable wrap

spicy vegetable wrap

serves
4

Q

V

4 soft wheat flour tortillas

harissa (optional)

2 carrots, grated

1 courgette, grated

2 spring onions, finely chopped

75 g sun-blushed tomatoes

8 iceberg lettuce leaves, chopped

The heat in this wrap comes from harissa, a red chilli paste from Morocco. If you are not that keen on very spicy food, simply leave it out or replace it with humous or Marmite.

Spread the tortillas sparingly with a little harissa, if using, leaving a 2-cm border around the edge. Sprinkle with a layer of grated carrot, then layers of courgette, spring onions, tomatoes and lettuce.

Roll the tortilla up tightly into a cigar shape. Cut in half across the middle and eat immediately or wrap in clingfilm until you are ready.

scrambled eggs

6 eggs

4 tablespoons milk

30 g butter

salt and black pepper

chopped chives, to serve

hot buttered toast

There are two ways of cooking scrambled eggs: in the microwave or on the hob in a non-stick pan. The second method is better because the eggs become creamy and delicious.

Whisk the eggs together with the milk and add salt and pepper. Melt the butter in a medium non-stick pan, then add the egg mixture, stirring frequently until it reaches a creamy consistency. Serve with a sprinkling of chopped chives and hot buttered toast.

scrambled eggs

*baked brunch
omelette*

baked *brunch* omelette

This is a great way to cook an omelette – once prepared, it can finish cooking in the oven, so you can get on with something else. Make sure the pan handle is ovenproof or removable.

Preheat the oven to 200°C (400°F) Gas 6.

Heat the oil in the frying pan, add the bacon, onion and potato and fry for 6 minutes, or until the potatoes start to brown. Add the mushrooms and fry for 2 minutes.

Meanwhile put the eggs and milk in a large bowl and whisk briefly with a fork, just enough to mix the yolks and whites. Season with salt and plenty of pepper. Stir in three-quarters of the Cheddar.

Using a slotted spoon, transfer the potato mixture to the bowl of eggs and mix well. Add the butter to the frying pan and, when it starts to foam, pour in the omelette mixture. Sprinkle with the remaining cheese and transfer to the preheated oven. Cook for 12–15 minutes, or until just set. Loosen the edges with a spatula or palette knife and slide onto a serving plate.

serves
2–3

M

2 tablespoons sunflower oil

4 rashers of smoked bacon, cut into strips

1 onion, finely sliced

1 potato, cubed

75 g button mushrooms, sliced

5 large eggs

90 ml milk

75 g mature Cheddar, grated

1 tablespoon butter

salt and black pepper

a 20-cm heavy non-stick frying pan (measure the base, not the top)

farmhouse sauté with *bacon* and *onions*

A great late-night feast for a gang of friends. You'll need some leftover cooked potatoes.

Heat the olive oil in a large frying pan over medium heat. Add the sliced cooked potatoes and fry on each side until golden. Remove the potatoes with a slotted spoon and set aside to drain on kitchen paper.

Add the onion, bacon and thyme to the frying pan and cook, stirring constantly, until the mixture is crisp and golden. Add the cooked potatoes and salt and pepper to taste. Mix well and serve at once.

serves
4

Q

M

3 tablespoons olive oil

1 kg cooked potatoes, thickly sliced

2 onions, diced

175 g bacon, chopped

3 sprigs of fresh thyme

salt and black pepper

sausage and bacon rolls

16 thin rashers of
streaky bacon

a little mustard

8 sausages

olive oil, for brushing

4 warm buttered soft rolls
or even small naan bread
or pita bread

tomato ketchup, to serve

serves
4

Q

M

There's nothing quite like a warm sausage-filled roll. Dotting
the sausages with mustard and wrapping them in bacon just
adds to the taste experience and the cooking smells will waken
even the most hungover. Get these under way while you make
a big pot of tea or coffee.

Preheat the grill.

Spread a little mustard over each slice of bacon. Wrap 2 slices around each
sausage. Put the sausages on the rack of a grilling pan so that the loose
ends of the bacon are underneath the sausage. Brush with a little oil and
grill for about 6–8 minutes on each side, depending on the thickness of the
sausage, until the bacon is crisp and the sausage cooked through. Serve in
buttered rolls with plenty of ketchup.

cheat's mini pizzas

4 English muffins

150 g passata (sieved
tomatoes)

toppings of your choice,
such as diced ham,
pineapple, sweetcorn,
flaked tuna, sliced
mushrooms, peppers and
shredded fresh herbs, etc.

50 g mozzarella or Cheddar,
grated

serves
4

Q

These ultra-quick pizzas are the answer to fast food when faced
with mates so hungry they simply can't wait for the real thing.
Passata is just shop-bought sieved tomatoes – perfect as an
instant tomato sauce, but if you have tinned chopped tomatoes
or even jarred tomato sauce left over from last night's pasta,
that will do too. Top the pizzas with anything you like!

Preheat the oven to 200°C (400°F) Gas 6.

Slice the muffins in half horizontally. Spread the passata over them, then
top with any toppings of your choice, or simply with a little grated cheese.

Bake in the preheated oven for 8–10 minutes until the muffins are crispy
round the edges and the cheese is golden and bubbling.

sausage and
bacon rolls

baked *sweet potatoes* with *lentils* and *bacon*

2 sweet potatoes,
about 100 g each

100 g red split lentils

220 ml hot vegetable stock

1 garlic clove, crushed

½ onion, very finely chopped

1 celery stalk,
very thinly sliced

½ tablespoon soy sauce

1 tablespoon tomato purée

3 rashers of bacon, grilled
and chopped

50 g extra mature Cheddar,
grated

an ovenproof dish

serves
2

M

Sweet potatoes and lentils are low-glycaemic index foods, which means they release their sugars into the blood stream at a slow and steady rate, helping to keep your energy levels constant. So although this is essentially a cheesy baked potato, it's much healthier, and it will keep you going for longer. For maximum ease, top the sweet potato with baked beans instead.

Preheat the oven to 200°C (400°F) Gas 6.

Lightly prick the sweet potatoes with a fork and bake directly on the shelves of the preheated oven for 35–40 minutes until soft when gently squeezed. Remove and leave until cool enough to handle.

Meanwhile, put the lentils in a saucepan, add the stock and bring to the boil. Cover, reduce the heat and simmer for 20–25 minutes until soft. Add more stock or water if the lentils start to dry out.

Meanwhile, put the garlic, onion, celery, soy sauce and 3–4 tablespoons water in a non-stick frying pan and heat gently for about 10 minutes or until the vegetables are soft. Add them to the saucepan of cooked lentils along with the tomato purée, chopped grilled bacon and half the grated cheese. Mix well, then reheat gently, stirring occasionally, until hot.

Turn off the oven and preheat the grill.

Cut the cooked sweet potatoes in half. Put them in an ovenproof dish and top with the lentil mixture. Sprinkle with the remaining cheese and cook under the hot grill for 10 minutes or until the cheese is golden and bubbling.

Note To cook the sweet potatoes in a microwave, wrap them in kitchen paper and cook each one individually on HIGH for 4–4½ minutes. Leave for 1 minute before topping with the lentils and grilling as in the recipe above.

potato wedges with *garlic* and *paprika*

Potatoes any way are great, but there's something particularly appealing about wedges. These have a delicious spice mix coating. Take a bowl of mayonnaise and stir in a bit of crushed garlic for dunking the wedges. Hard to imagine anything better.

serves
4

V

1.5 kg potatoes, unpeeled but well scrubbed

1 dried bay leaf (optional)

5 tablespoons olive oil

3 garlic cloves, crushed

1 tablespoon dried oregano

1 teaspoon paprika

salt and black pepper

If the potatoes are large, cut in half lengthways, otherwise leave whole. Put in a large saucepan of water with the bay leaf (if using). When the water boils, add a heaped tablespoon of salt and cook until just tender, but not completely soft. Drain and leave to cool slightly.

When the potatoes are cool enough to handle, cut into wedges. Put in a large dish and add the oil, garlic, oregano, paprika and salt and mix well.

Preheat the oven to 230°C (450°F) Gas 8.

Arrange the wedges in a single layer on a baking tray and bake in the preheated oven until browned, 30–40 minutes. Sprinkle with pepper.

baked sweet potatoes with lentils and bacon

potato wedges with garlic and paprika

*sesame sweet
potato wedges*

sesame *sweet potato* wedges

This nutty dipping sauce works brilliantly with the sweetness of the potatoes. Serve them with with very cold beer when friends come round for an evening in front of the telly.

Preheat the oven to 200°C (400°F) Gas 6.

Arrange the sweet potato wedges in a single layer on the baking tray, then sprinkle with the olive and sesame oils, sesame seeds and salt. Roast in the preheated oven for 35 minutes or until tender (the cooking time will vary depending on the size of the wedges).

Meanwhile, to prepare the dipping sauce, put the peanut butter, lime juice, chilli, soy sauce and tomato ketchup in a bowl with 4 tablespoons hot water and stir until smooth. Add salt and pepper to taste, then pour into a saucepan and heat gently.

Sprinkle the wedges with coriander and serve with a separate bowl of the dipping sauce.

Note To simplify this recipe even further, serve the wedges with shop-bought sweet chilli sauce.

serves
6–8

V

750 g sweet potatoes, well scrubbed but unpeeled, cut lengthways into thick wedges

2 tablespoons olive oil

1 tablespoon toasted sesame oil

1 tablespoon sesame seeds

torn fresh coriander, to serve

salt and black pepper

Dipping sauce

2 tablespoons peanut butter

1 tablespoon lime juice

½ red chilli, deseeded and very finely chopped

1 tablespoon soy sauce

1 tablespoon tomato ketchup

a baking tray

creamy *mustard* mash

Mashed potato with mustard is true comfort food. For a change, try adding grated cheese, chopped herbs and fried onions.

Put the potatoes in a saucepan of water, bring to the boil, then lower the heat and simmer for 20 minutes or until tender. Drain the cooked potatoes thoroughly, then return them to the pan and set it over low heat. Shake the pan and let the potatoes steam dry.

Put the milk, olive oil and butter in a separate saucepan and warm gently.

Mash the potatoes well, being sure to crush out all the lumps.

Add the warm milk mixture, mustard, salt and pepper to the mashed potatoes. Using a wooden spoon, beat well until smooth and well blended. Taste and season with salt and pepper as necessary.

serves
4

V

750 g potatoes, cut into large cubes

150 ml milk

3 tablespoons olive oil

50 g butter

1 tablespoon English mustard powder

salt and black pepper

rosemary potatoes

1 kg floury potatoes (such as Maris Piper or King Edward), peeled and cut into small chunks

4 tablespoons olive oil

2 garlic cloves, crushed

a small handful of fresh rosemary needles, chopped

salt and black pepper

a roasting tin

serves
4

V

Potatoes roasted with rosemary and garlic are heavenly. They are the perfect accompaniment to a Sunday roast.

Preheat the oven to 200°C (400°F) Gas 6.

Put the potatoes in a bowl, cover with water and leave them to soak for 10 minutes, then drain and pat dry with kitchen paper.

Pour the olive oil into a roasting tin and put it in the preheated oven. Heat for 3–4 minutes until the oil is hot.

Remove the tin from the oven, add the potatoes and return the tin to the oven. Roast the potatoes for about 35 minutes, until crisp and golden and almost soft.

Remove the tin from the oven and scatter the garlic, rosemary and some salt and black pepper over the potatoes. Stir and return to the oven for 5–10 minutes longer. Drain the potatoes on kitchen paper before serving.

bubble and *squeak* patties

100 g Savoy cabbage, shredded

250 g potatoes, peeled, cooked and mashed

50 g mature Cheddar, grated

1½ teaspoons Dijon mustard

1 small egg, lightly beaten

plain flour, for dusting

2 tablespoons sunflower or rapeseed oil

salt and black pepper

makes
6

Q

V

This is a great way of using up leftover mashed potatoes. Serve the patties with grilled tomatoes and meat or vegetarian sausages. They're also good cold as a snack.

Steam or boil the cabbage for 2–3 minutes until just tender. Leave to cool, then squeeze out any excess water using your hands.

Finely chop the cabbage, then put it in a bowl with the mashed potato, cheese and Dijon mustard. Season to taste and mix until combined, then stir in the egg. Divide the mixture into 6. Using floured hands, form each portion into a patty shape. Lightly dust each patty with flour.

Pour the oil into a large non-stick frying pan and heat. Cook 3 patties at a time for 3–4 minutes each side until golden, adding a little more oil if necessary. Keep the cakes that you've cooked warm while you cook the rest. Drain the patties on kitchen paper to remove any excess oil before serving.

rosemary potatoes

*potato skins
with green dip*

potato skins with green dip

This recipe makes a lot of potato skins but they are so moreish that you'll be glad you made this many.

Preheat the oven to 180°C (350°F) Gas 4.

Using a sharp knife, pierce each potato right through the middle. Bake in the preheated oven for about 1 hour 10 minutes or until cooked through. Remove and set aside until cool enough to handle. Raise the heat to 220°C (425°F) Gas 7. Cut each potato in half lengthways and scoop out the potato middles, leaving a thin layer lining the skin. Cut each skin into 4 wedges. Brush oil over the potato skins and arrange in a single layer on the prepared baking tray. Bake at the top of the oven for 30 minutes, moving the potatoes around occasionally to ensure even cooking. Remove from the oven and reduce the heat to 200°C (400°F) Gas 6. Sprinkle with cheese and return to the oven for 5–10 minutes until the cheese is melted.

To make the dip, put the soured cream, chives, spring onions and parsley into a bowl. Add salt and pepper to taste and mix well.

makes
24

V

3 large baking potatoes

50 ml olive oil

100 g mature Cheddar, grated

Green dip

100 ml soured cream

a handful of fresh chives, snipped

3 spring onions, chopped

a bunch of fresh flat leaf parsley, chopped

salt and black pepper

a baking tray, lightly greased

three-cheese *cauliflower*

How can you improve on this classic comfort food? Use a variety of high-end cheeses to make it even richer.

Preheat the oven to 190°C (375°F) Gas 5.

Plunge the cauliflower florets into a saucepan of boiling water. Bring back to the boil, then simmer for 4 minutes and drain well.

Put the cheeses in a bowl, sprinkle in the cornflour and mix to coat the cheese evenly. Transfer to a non-stick saucepan, add 200 ml water and gently bring to a slight simmer, stirring constantly until you have a smooth sauce.

Put the cauliflower in the ovenproof dish and pour the cheese sauce all over it. Bake in the preheated oven for 15 minutes, until golden on top. Take care when serving as the cheese gets extremely hot.

serves
4

V

1 cauliflower, cut into florets

100 g Gruyère, grated

100 g Emmenthal, grated

100 g Beaufort or other hard, strong cheese, grated

1 teaspoon cornflour

salt and black pepper

a shallow ovenproof dish, about 20 x 26 cm

broccoli cheese

500 g broccoli, cut into florets

4 tablespoons sunflower oil

4 tablespoons plain flour

400 ml milk

75 g mature Cheddar, grated, plus extra for sprinkling

an ovenproof dish

serves
4

V

A little like the Three-cheese Cauliflower on page 49, only with a lot less cheese for a lighter conscience.

Preheat the grill.

Steam the broccoli over gently simmering water for 8 minutes or until it is tender but still has some bite. Drain and transfer to the ovenproof dish.

Heat the oil in a small saucepan and stir in the flour. Cook, stirring, for 2 minutes. Remove the pan from the heat and gradually stir in the milk. Return the pan to the heat and cook, stirring continuously, until the sauce thickens. Add the grated cheese and stir until melted. Pour the sauce over the broccoli and sprinkle with a little more grated cheese. Cook under the grill for 10–15 minutes until the cheese is golden brown and bubbling.

stir-fried *sesame cabbage*

2 tablespoons peanut oil

1 tablespoon toasted sesame oil

2 garlic cloves, sliced

1 red chilli, deseeded and sliced

1 kg Savoy cabbage, finely shredded

1 tablespoon chopped fresh coriander

juice of ½ a lemon

50 g dry-roasted peanuts

2 tablespoons sesame seeds, lightly toasted in a dry frying pan

salt and black pepper

serves
4

Q

V

Soggy old boiled cabbage – no way, this quick stir-fried dish is crunchy, spicy and lemony and makes an ideal accompaniment to pork dishes, or as a quick veggie snack by itself.

Heat the two oils together in a wok or large, deep frying pan, add the garlic and chilli and stir-fry over high heat for 30 seconds.

Add the cabbage and stir-fry for a further 2–3 minutes until golden and the cabbage is starting to soften.

Add the coriander, lemon juice, peanuts, sesame seeds, salt and pepper, stir well and transfer to a warmed dish. Serve at once.

broccoli cheese

*rice noodle salad
with prawns*

cannellini beans with *garlic* and *parsley*

These make such an easy and delicious side dish. If you like, you could leave them without heating and serve them as a small salad or pick-me-up before heading out for the evening.

Put the beans in a saucepan and add the onion, garlic, olive oil and half the parsley. Season with salt and pepper and stir gently but thoroughly. Set aside for about 30 minutes to allow the flavours to develop.

Heat the beans gently until warm. Stir in the remaining parsley and drizzle with a little extra olive oil.

serves 6

V

2 x 400-g tins cannellini beans, drained and rinsed

1 small onion, finely chopped

2 garlic cloves, crushed

100 ml olive oil, plus extra to serve

4 tablespoons fresh parsley leaves, finely chopped

salt and black pepper

rice noodle salad with *prawns*

A delicious and sustaining lunch. If you'd like to spice it up a little more, add some chopped spring onions, fresh coriander and red chilli.

Cook the noodles according to the packet instructions. Drain, toss them in a little of the oil and leave to cool in the colander for 10 minutes.

Heat the remaining oil in a wok or large frying pan and add the ginger, garlic, prawns, beans and carrot. Cook over a medium heat for 4 minutes, stirring constantly. Add the mixture to the cooled noodles and mix well. Sprinkle with cashew nuts and toasted sesame seeds.

serves 6

Q

F

150 g thin rice noodles

2 tablespoons vegetable oil

1 cm fresh ginger, peeled and finely chopped

1 garlic clove, crushed

175 g cooked peeled prawns

50 g fine green beans, trimmed

1 carrot, cut into matchsticks

juice of ½ a lime

50 g cashew nuts, chopped

1 tablespoon sesame seeds, lightly toasted in a dry frying pan

100 g dried pasta,
such as penne

1 red onion, thinly sliced

3 celery stalks, chopped

1 carrot, grated

50 g sultanas

8-cm piece of cucumber,
chopped

50 g tinned sweetcorn

400 g tinned tuna, drained
and flaked

6 tablespoons mayonnaise

6 tablespoons Greek yoghurt

salad leaves

225 g cherry tomatoes, halved

tuna pasta salad

This is a good idea for a hurried lunch, but it's also ideal for
making in advance and popping in a container for lunch later on.

Cook the pasta in a large saucepan of boiling water for 12–15 minutes, or
according to the manufacturer's instructions, until al dente. Drain, refresh
under cold running water and transfer to a large bowl.

Cut the onion slices in half to form half moons, then add to the bowl along
with the celery, carrot, sultanas, cucumber, sweetcorn and tuna.

Mix the mayonnaise with the yoghurt and add it to the salad. Stir gently
until well coated. (You can make the recipe up to this point and store,
covered, in the refrigerator for up to 2 days.)

To serve, line a plate with salad leaves, put a serving of the pasta salad
on top and scatter over a few halved tomatoes.

125 g white cabbage,
shredded

125 g red cabbage, shredded

175 g carrots, grated

½ onion, thinly sliced

2 teaspoons caster sugar

1 tablespoon white wine
vinegar

50 ml mayonnaise

50 g soured cream

salt and black pepper

soured cream coleslaw

You could use single rather than soured cream if you like here,
but the sharp flavour of soured cream works particularly well.

Put the white and red cabbage, carrots and onion in a colander and
sprinkle with the salt, sugar and vinegar. Stir well and leave to drain over
a bowl for 20 minutes.

Transfer the vegetables to a clean tea towel and squeeze out any excess
liquid. Put them in a large bowl and stir in the mayonnaise and cream.
Season to taste with salt and pepper and serve.

greek
country
salad

greek country salad

Choose very ripe tomatoes that are still firm but full of flavour. Splash out on beefsteak tomatoes, or those on the vine, if you can, as they will be more flavourful.

Cut the tomatoes into wedges. Put them in a large bowl along with the lettuce, cucumber, olives and feta, if using.

Put all the dressing ingredients in a bowl, whisk well with a fork, then drizzle over the salad and toss well to coat evenly. Sprinkle with the oregano and serve at once.

serves
4

Q

V

4 tomatoes

1 cos lettuce heart, sliced

2 small cucumbers, sliced

100 g stoned black olives

200 g feta, crumbled (optional)

1 teaspoon dried oregano

Dressing

4 tablespoons olive oil

4 teaspoons red wine vinegar

½ teaspoon caster sugar

salt and black pepper

easy mains

scotch broth

scotch *broth*

Barley is traditionally used in scotch broth, but here we have brown rice in its place. And it goes without saying that soy sauce is never used in traditional Scottish fare but it works well with the other flavours in this recipe. This broth is dead simple, with a minimum of ingredients, but you could add some herbs if you like. Thyme, in particular, likes being with lamb.

Heat the oil in a large saucepan. Add the carrot, leek, celery stalks and leaves and cook over high heat for 5 minutes, stirring often. Add the lamb, stock, soy sauce, rice and 1 litre water and bring to the boil.

Reduce the heat to low, cover with a tight-fitting lid and leave the soup to simmer for 1 hour. Season to taste with salt and pepper and serve with soft, buttered rolls on the side.

serves 4

M

2 tablespoons olive oil

1 carrot, diced

1 leek, diced

2 celery stalks, diced and leaves chopped

500 g stewing lamb, well trimmed of fat and cubed

500 ml chicken stock

1 tablespoon light soy sauce

95 g brown rice

salt and black pepper

4 soft rolls, buttered, to serve

soup with *pasta shells, peas, artichokes* and *chilli*

An incredibly speedy soup that has a wonderful, fresh flavour, yet is made almost entirely from storecupboard ingredients. Enjoy a taste of summer all year round.

Heat the oil in a large saucepan, add the onion, garlic, chilli and bacon and cook for 4–5 minutes until golden.

Add the oregano, artichokes and peas and stir-fry for 2 minutes. Add the stock, bring to the boil, then simmer for 10 minutes.

Meanwhile, bring another large saucepan of water to the boil. Add a good pinch of salt, then the pasta, and cook until al dente, or according to the manufacturer's instructions.

Drain the pasta and add it to the soup. Pour into bowls, sprinkle with Parmesan, then serve.

serves 4

Q

M

1 tablespoon olive oil

1 onion, finely chopped

2 garlic cloves, crushed

2 red chillies, thinly sliced

4 rashers of smoked streaky bacon, finely chopped

1 teaspoon dried oregano

400-g tin artichoke hearts in water, drained and quartered

100 g frozen peas

1.25 litres hot chicken or vegetable stock

75 g any dried pasta shapes

salt and black pepper

2 tablespoons grated Parmesan, to serve

chunky *chickpea* soup

2 tablespoons olive oil

1 leek, thinly sliced

1 small fennel bulb, diced

100 g pancetta, diced

1 carrot, grated

1 potato, diced

1.5 litres hot chicken or vegetable stock

400-g tin chickpeas, rinsed and drained

80 g fresh spinach, chopped

50 g grated Parmesan

salt and black pepper

serves
4

M

This version of minestrone is a meal in its own right. Packed with winter vegetables, it's a 'one-pot wonder' that improves with age. Pancetta is available ready chopped and pre-packed.

Heat the oil in a saucepan. Add the leek, fennel and pancetta and cook for 5 minutes over high heat, until the leek softens and the pancetta really flavours the oil. Add the carrot, potato, stock and chickpeas and bring to the boil. Reduce the heat and simmer for 20 minutes. Season to taste with salt and pepper, then add the spinach. Cook over low heat for 5 minutes, until the spinach has wilted throughout the soup.

Serve with Parmesan sprinkled over the top.

Variation Add 100 g small pasta (try the little rice-shaped pastas such as risoni or orzo) instead of chickpeas and simmer until the pasta is cooked through before adding the final few ingredients. This will give you a very thick soup that you may even need a fork to eat!

vegetable, ham and barley broth

1 tablespoon sunflower oil

2 onions, sliced

100 g pearl barley, rinsed

1 celery stalk, sliced

1.2 litres hot chicken or vegetable stock

2 dried bay leaves

a sprig of fresh thyme

2 large carrots, halved lengthways and sliced

1 sweet potato, peeled and cut into bite-sized chunks

200 g thickly cut cooked ham, diced, or 100 g tinned chickpeas, drained and rinsed

salt and black pepper

serves
4

M

This nurturing broth makes a nutritious light lunch, supper or between-meal snack. It is filling enough to be served on its own, but if you are feeling really peckish, you could have it with a slice of bread and a chunk of Cheddar.

Heat the oil in a large saucepan and sauté the onions, half-covered, for 5 minutes. Add the barley and stir so that it is coated in the oil. Cook for another 2 minutes, stirring continuously.

Add the celery, stock, bay leaves and thyme to the pan. Bring to the boil, then reduce the heat and simmer, half-covered, for 30 minutes, occasionally skimming away with a large spoon any froth from the barley that rises to the surface.

Add the carrots, sweet potato and ham and cook for another 15–20 minutes until the vegetables and barley are tender. Season with salt and pepper to taste, then remove the bay leaves and thyme before serving.

chunky
chickpea
soup

chickpea, tomato and chorizo soup

chickpea, tomato and chorizo soup

This soup tastes fantastic and is refreshingly simple to prepare. Make sure you buy the correct chorizo – you want the short, fat cured sausages. They are ready to eat but are much better fried.

Put the chorizo in a large saucepan over medium heat and cook until it starts to release its oil. Continue to cook, stirring, for 4–5 minutes until it is lovely and crisp. Add the red onion and garlic and turn the heat right down to allow them to soften in the chorizo's paprika-infused oil. After 6–7 minutes the onion and garlic should be translucent and glossy. Add the tomatoes and thyme and turn the heat back up. Cook for 5 minutes to intensify the flavour, then add the chickpeas and stock. Return to the boil, cover and simmer for 15 minutes.

Remove the thyme. Season well with salt and pepper and simmer for a further 10 minutes to allow all the flavours to get to know one another. Transfer to bowls and serve.

serves
4

M

200 g cured chorizo, roughly chopped

1 red onion, chopped

2 garlic cloves, crushed

400-g tin chopped tomatoes

2 fresh thyme sprigs

400-g tin chickpeas, drained and rinsed

1 litre hot vegetable stock

salt and black pepper

split pea and sausage soup

The thick wintry mix of tender lentils with chunks of sausage in this soup is so filling, it's almost a casserole – perfect to get you ready for a long walk, or maybe just a long snooze on the sofa.

Heat the olive oil in a large saucepan and cook the onion, leek and celery gently over low heat for 8–10 minutes. Add the nutmeg and stir in. Add the split peas and mix into the vegetables. Add the stock and bay leaves, cover and simmer for 45 minutes or until the peas are tender and beginning to get mushy when pressed with the back of a spoon.

Meanwhile, preheat the grill.

Grill the sausages until cooked, then roughly chop. Add to the soup and cook for a further 10 minutes. Season with salt and pepper and serve.

serves
6

M

2 tablespoons olive oil

1 onion, chopped

1 leek, chopped

2 celery stalks, chopped

a pinch of grated nutmeg

300 g yellow split peas

1.5 litres hot chicken stock

2 dried bay leaves

250 g sausages

salt and black pepper

40 g butter

150 g pancetta or smoked bacon, cubed

1 onion, sliced

2 carrots, finely chopped

300 g new potatoes (unpeeled), thinly sliced

2 tablespoons plain flour

600 ml milk

400 ml hot chicken or vegetable stock

3 dried bay leaves

300 g sweetcorn (defrosted if frozen)

3 tablespoons double cream

salt and black pepper

sweetcorn and *pancetta* chowder

Although there are many variations, a chowder is often a creamy stock thickened with potatoes and spiked with the rich flavour of smoky bacon. This one is bowl food of the most warming and comforting kind. Roaring fire optional.

Heat the butter in a large saucepan and fry the pancetta until crisp. Add the onion, carrots and potatoes, cover and cook gently for 15–20 minutes until soft. Stir occasionally.

Sprinkle the flour into the pan and cook for 1 minute, stirring it into the vegetables. Pour in the milk gradually, blending it with the flour, then add the stock and bay leaves; bring to a gentle simmer. Add the sweetcorn and cook for 5 minutes.

Remove from the heat, stir in the cream and season with salt. Pour into bowls and serve with a fresh grinding of pepper

1.4 litres warm chicken stock

100 g long grain rice

400 g cooked chicken, shredded

3 eggs

juice of 1 lemon

croutons, to serve

chicken avgolemono

Use up any chicken you might have left over after a slap-up Sunday roast, or buy some pre-cooked chicken from the supermarket. Either way, this soup requires minimum effort.

Heat the stock in a large saucepan and add the rice. Bring to the boil and simmer for 15 minutes or until the rice is tender. Add the chicken and warm through for 2–3 minutes.

In the meantime, whisk the eggs and lemon juice in a small bowl. Add a ladleful of the warm stock and whisk until thinned. Remove the soup from the heat and gradually pour in the egg mixture, whisking to amalgamate it. It should thicken in the residual heat, but if you need to, place it over low heat for just 3–4 minutes, stirring the bottom of the pan to thicken. Do not return to high heat once the egg has been added, or it will scramble.

Pour the soup into bowls and garnish with croutons.

sweetcorn and
pancetta chowder

spaghetti bolognese

Like many classic, handed-down recipes, there are countless versions of Bolognese sauce. This one uses minced beef and Parma ham, as well as dried porcini mushrooms, which may seem extravagant but try it and see – it's worth the extra little ingredients to make it taste this good. It benefits from being chilled overnight, so it tastes even better the second time round.

serves
4

M

10 g dried porcini
mushrooms, rinsed

1 tablespoon olive oil

1 onion, finely chopped

500 g minced beef

50 g Parma ham,
coarsely chopped

100 ml Marsala or sherry

700 ml tomato passata
(sieved tomatoes)

300 g dried pasta,
such as spaghetti or linguine

salt and black pepper

Parmesan shavings, to serve

Put the porcini into a bowl, cover with boiling water and set aside for 20 minutes until softened.

Heat the oil in a large saucepan, add the onion and cook for 2 minutes. Add the minced beef and Parma ham and cook for 3–4 minutes, stirring, until evenly browned.

Drain the porcini and discard the soaking water. Chop the porcini, then add to the pan with the Marsala and passata. Cover and simmer for 1 hour, stirring occasionally, until rich and dark. Add salt and pepper to taste.

Meanwhile, bring a large saucepan of water to the boil. Add a good pinch of salt, then the pasta, and cook until al dente, or according to the manufacturer's instructions.

Drain the pasta and transfer to plates or bowls. Top with the Bolognese sauce and Parmesan shavings, then serve.

pasta with *puttanesca sauce*

serves
4

F

2 tablespoons olive oil

1 onion, finely chopped

2 garlic cloves, crushed

4 anchovy fillets in oil,
drained and chopped

2 red chillies, finely chopped

4 ripe tomatoes, chopped

1 tablespoon salted capers,
rinsed well and chopped

100 ml red wine

350 g dried pasta, such as
penne or rigatoni

75 g small stoned black olives

2 tablespoons chopped fresh
flat leaf parsley

black pepper

grated Parmesan, to serve

Puttanesca sauce is chilli-hot, with a salty depth from anchovies and capers. More importantly, it's a great excuse to crack open a bottle of red wine, a little of which you need in this recipe.

Heat the oil in a saucepan, then add the onion, garlic, anchovies and chillies. Cook over medium heat for 4–5 minutes until softened and golden. Add the tomatoes and cook for 3–4 minutes, stirring occasionally, until softened. Add the capers, wine and pepper to taste, then cover and simmer for 20 minutes.

Meanwhile, bring a large saucepan of water to the boil. Add a good pinch of salt, then the pasta, and cook until al dente, or according to the manufacturer's instructions.

Drain well and return the pasta to the warm pan. Add the tomato sauce, olives and parsley and toss to mix. Transfer to bowls and serve topped with grated Parmesan.

white *spaghetti*

serves
2

Q

F

150 g dried pasta,
such as spaghetti

6 tablespoons olive oil

4 garlic cloves, halved

6 anchovy fillets
in oil, drained

salt and black pepper

This is one of those dishes that saves your life when you get home tired and hungry. Always keep some anchovies, olive oil and spaghetti in the cupboard to make this at short notice.

Bring a large saucepan of water to the boil. Add a good pinch of salt, then the pasta, and cook until al dente, or according to the manufacturer's instructions.

Put the olive oil and garlic in a small saucepan and heat very gently over low heat for 4–5 minutes until the garlic is pale golden but not browned. Remove and discard the garlic. Add the anchovies and 100 ml water to the pan and simmer rapidly, whisking with the fork until the anchovies have almost dissolved into the mixture. Add plenty of pepper and a tiny pinch of salt. Drain the pasta and return it to the warm pan. Add the anchovy mixture and toss well to mix. Transfer to bowls and serve.

*pasta with
puttanesca sauce*

*fusilli with
sausage ragu*

*tuscan tuna
and bean pasta*

fusilli with *sausage ragu*

serves
4–6

M

Chorizo, the spicy Spanish sausage, is used in this rich ragu, but you could substitute any Italian-style sausage if you prefer.

400–500 g dried pasta, such as fusilli

750 g raw chorizo sausage

2 tablespoons olive oil

1 onion, finely chopped

2 garlic cloves, crushed

2 tablespoons chopped fresh sage

2 x 400-g tins chopped tomatoes

125 ml red wine

2 tablespoons tomato purée

2 tablespoons chopped fresh flat leaf parsley

salt and black pepper

Bring a large saucepan of water to the boil. Add a good pinch of salt, then the pasta, and cook until al dente, or according to the manufacturer's instructions.

Cut away the skins of the sausages and finely chop the sausagemeat.

Heat the olive oil in a saucepan and gently fry the onion, garlic, sage and salt and pepper over low heat for 10 minutes, or until soft and lightly golden. Add the sausagemeat and stir-fry over medium heat for 5 minutes, or until browned. Add the tinned tomatoes, wine and tomato purée, bring to the boil, cover and simmer gently for 1 hour, or until the sauce has thickened. Season with salt and pepper to taste, stir in the parsley and serve.

tuscan *tuna* and *bean* pasta

This is the fastest, easiest pasta sauce you can make and it's so filling it can be served as a meal in itself with some crusty bread. Make the whole amount, even if it's just for yourself, then refrigerate the rest in an airtight container for tomorrow, or freeze it for another time.

Bring a large saucepan of water to the boil. Add a good pinch of salt, then the pasta, and cook until al dente, or according to the manufacturer's instructions.

Meanwhile, put the tomatoes, tuna, beans, stock, coriander, and salt and pepper in a saucepan and heat, stirring occasionally, for about 5 minutes until piping hot. Spoon the sauce over the pasta, stir and serve.

Note If you have a food processor or stick blender, you can purée the ingredients together first before heating them up in a saucepan.

serves
6

Q

F

500 g dried pasta, such as penne

400-g tin chopped tomatoes

200 g tinned tuna, drained

300 g tinned beans, such as red kidney, butter bean or haricot, drained and rinsed

100 ml hot vegetable stock

1 tablespoon chopped fresh coriander

salt and black pepper

cherry tomato puttanesca sauce

Here's another version of the Puttanesca Sauce from page 68. This one is made using cherry tomatoes to add extra texture and a slightly sweeter flavour.

Heat the olive oil in a large frying pan and gently fry the garlic, chilli flakes and seasoning for 3–4 minutes, or until softened. Add the tomatoes, stir-fry for 1 minute, then stir in the olives, anchovies, capers, lemon juice and basil and heat through. Serve topped with grated cheese, if desired.

serves
4

Q

F

4 tablespoons olive oil

2 garlic cloves, crushed

a pinch of dried chilli flakes

500 g cherry tomatoes, halved

100 g stoned black olives, halved

6 anchovy fillets in oil, drained and chopped

4 tablespoons capers in brine, drained and washed

juice of 1 lemon

2 tablespoons chopped fresh basil

salt and black pepper

grated cheese, to serve

rigatoni with *bacon* and *beans*

Rustic and hearty, this pasta dish makes a warming supper. Tinned beans are a convenient storecupboard standby, plus nutritionists say that three heaped tablespoons of beans count as a single portion of the recommended 'five-a-day' so you can dish up a generous helping knowing that you're doing good!

serves
2

M

1 tablespoon olive oil

1 onion, chopped

1 garlic clove, crushed

1 teaspoon dried oregano

140 g smoked bacon, roughly chopped

400 ml passata (sieved tomatoes)

a pinch of sugar

1 teaspoon tomato purée

100 g tinned borlotti beans, drained and rinsed

200 g dried pasta, such as rigatoni or penne

salt and black pepper

Heat the oil in a saucepan and fry the onion for 8 minutes until softened, then stir in the garlic, oregano and bacon and cook for another 2 minutes.

Pour in the passata and stir in the sugar and tomato purée. Bring to the boil, then reduce the heat to low and simmer, half-covered, for 10 minutes, stirring occasionally. Add the beans, stir and cook for another 5 minutes.

Meanwhile, cook the pasta in plenty of boiling salted water, following the manufacturer's instructions, until al dente. Drain, reserving 4 tablespoons of the cooking water. Set aside.

Add the cooked pasta and reserved cooking water to the sauce and heat through before serving. Season with salt and pepper to taste.

Note There is a temptation, when you're short on cash and time, to turn to pasta for sustenance a little too often. Although pasta is not bad for you, it's not especially nutritious, so it's best to eat it in moderation, or at least in as healthy a form as possible. The recipe above is a good option, but you can also make any of the other pasta recipes in this book kinder to your diet by using wholemeal pasta and avoiding pairing it with unhealthy temptations, such as garlic bread.

prawn curry

serves
4

Q

F

Tiger prawns or large peeled prawns are ideal for this colourful, citrus-flavoured curry.

Cook the rice according to the manufacturer's instructions.

Meanwhile, heat the oil in a large pan, add the onion, garlic, ginger and chilli and cook for 5 minutes over medium heat. Add the turmeric, curry powder, ground coriander and cumin and mix well. Add the prawns and cook for 3 minutes.

Pour in the tomatoes and lime juice, season with salt and pepper and bring to the boil. Reduce the heat and simmer for 5 minutes. Serve with the rice.

200–250 g basmati rice

2 tablespoons vegetable oil

1 onion, grated

3 garlic cloves, crushed

5 cm fresh ginger, peeled and sliced

1 mild red chilli, chopped

1 teaspoon ground turmeric

2 teaspoons curry powder

1 teaspoon ground coriander

1 teaspoon ground cumin

400 g cooked peeled prawns

400-g tin chopped tomatoes

juice of 2 limes

indonesian fried rice

serves
4

Q

M

F

This beats takeaway egg fried rice hands down. And the great thing is you can use yesterday's leftover boiled rice. Remember to make sure the rice is piping hot when you serve it as it can be dangerous to eat partially reheated cooked rice.

Heat 2 tablespoons of the oil in a large frying pan until hot. Add the onion and stir-fry over high heat for 2–3 minutes, or until softened and golden. Add the garlic and continue to cook for 1 minute. Add the chilli sauce and shrimp paste and cook for 1 minute, then throw in the chicken. Stir-fry for 2 minutes, then add the prawns and cook until opaque and cooked through.

Throw in the carrot, sweetcorn and green beans and cook for 2 minutes, or until the beans are cooked but still crunchy. Add the rice and soy sauce to the wok and mix through. Cook until the rice is piping hot, then remove from the heat and set aside.

Heat the remaining oil in a large frying pan and pour in the beaten eggs. Leave to set into a thin omelette. Transfer to a wooden board and leave to cool for 1 minute. Roll up the omelette tightly and slice as thinly as possible. Transfer the fried rice to bowls and garnish with the omelette.

2½ tablespoons vegetable oil

1 small onion, finely chopped

2 garlic cloves, crushed

2 tablespoons chilli sauce

2 teaspoons shrimp paste

1 large skinless chicken breast fillet, about 220 g, diced

200 g uncooked peeled prawns, roughly chopped

100 g carrot, finely grated

200 g tinned sweetcorn

100 g green beans, trimmed and finely chopped

500 g cold, cooked basmati rice

1 tablespoon light soy sauce

2 large eggs, lightly beaten with a pinch of salt

prawn curry

thai green chicken curry

thai green *chicken* curry

There is a wonderful fragrance to Thai curries, and they make a fantastic shared meal. Build up the chilli content gradually until you find a spiciness that everyone enjoys.

serves
4

M

Heat the oil in a large saucepan, add the onion, ginger, garlic, lemongrass and chilli and cook over a low heat for 5 minutes. Add the chicken and cook for a further 5 minutes.

Add the kaffir lime leaves and curry paste and mix well. Shake the tin of coconut milk and slowly pour into the curry, mixing constantly. Pour in 100 ml water and the lime juice, bring to a simmer and cook gently for 5 minutes. Add the broccoli and beans and simmer for another 3 minutes. A large bowl of plain boiled jasmine rice is a good accompaniment.

2 tablespoons vegetable oil

1 onion, sliced

5 cm fresh ginger, peeled and sliced

2 garlic cloves, crushed

1 lemongrass stem, chopped

1 mild green chilli, diced

4 skinless chicken breast fillets, sliced

2 kaffir lime leaves

2 tablespoons Thai green curry paste

200-ml tin coconut milk

juice of 1 lime

75 g broccoli florets

75 g green beans, trimmed

salt and black pepper

indian *lamb* curry

This is a simple but unbeatable curry that needs plenty of time on the stove to produce meltingly soft lamb.

serves
4–6

M

Heat half the oil in a large pan, add the onion, ginger, chilli and garlic and cook over high heat for 1 minute, stirring constantly. Add the spices, then continue to cook for 1 minute. Transfer to a plate.

Heat the remaining tablespoon of oil in the pan and fry the lamb briskly until browned, about 5 minutes. Return the onion mixture to the pan and add the tomatoes. Season and pour in just enough water to cover. Bring to the boil, then lower the heat, cover and simmer for 1½–2 hours, stirring occasionally. The lamb should be tender and the sauce thick.

Just before serving, add the coriander. Plain boiled basmati rice is a good accompaniment, as is natural yoghurt to temper the heat of the curry.

2 tablespoons vegetable oil

1 onion, sliced

5 cm fresh ginger, peeled and chopped

1 mild red chilli, chopped

3 garlic cloves, crushed

1 teaspoon garam masala

1 teaspoon mild curry powder

800 g lamb neck fillet, cut into 3-cm pieces

400-g tin chopped tomatoes

a bunch of fresh coriander, chopped

salt and black pepper

chilli chicken enchiladas

3 tablespoons sunflower oil

450 g skinless chicken breast fillets, cut into strips

1 large onion, chopped

1 red chilli, deseeded and finely chopped

1 garlic clove, crushed

2 tablespoons tomato purée

400-g tin chopped tomatoes

410-g tin pinto beans, rinsed and drained

1 tablespoon chopped fresh coriander

8 corn tortillas, warmed

150 ml soured cream

75 g mature Cheddar, grated

salt and black pepper

shredded spring onions, to sprinkle

an ovenproof dish, lightly greased

serves
4–6

M

Corn tortillas, pinto beans and chillies are synonymous with Mexican cooking. This recipe combines chicken with a fiery tomato sauce as a filling for the soft tortillas, which are topped with soured cream and Cheddar before baking. It makes a perfect lunch or supper dish served with a crisp leaf salad.

Preheat the oven to 190°C (375°F) Gas 5.

Heat 2 tablespoons of the oil in a large non-stick frying pan, add the chicken and stir-fry for 4–5 minutes, or until golden. Remove with a slotted spoon, put into a bowl and set aside.

Add the remaining oil to the pan, then the onion and fry for 5 minutes. Add the chilli and garlic and fry for 1–2 minutes more, or until the onions are soft and golden. Stir in the tomato purée, tinned tomatoes and 100 ml cold water. Cook for 2–3 minutes and season with salt and pepper.

Add just under half the sauce to the chicken with the beans and coriander and mix together. Spoon 2 heaped tablespoons of the chicken mixture onto the middle of each warmed tortilla and roll up to enclose the filling. Place seam-side down in the prepared ovenproof dish and top with the remaining tomato sauce.

Spoon the soured cream along the centre of the tortillas and sprinkle with the grated cheese. Bake in the preheated oven for 15–20 minutes or until golden and bubbling. Sprinkle over the spring onions and serve.

*chicken lemon
skewers*

chicken lemon skewers

If you can, cook these skewers on a barbecue – the yoghurt becomes delicious and slightly crunchy. Failing that, they are delicious under the grill, indoors on a cloudy day, to give you a taste of sunshine. Note that they need to marinate overnight in the fridge before cooking.

Cut the chicken fillets lengthways into 2-mm thick strips and put into a shallow ceramic dish. Put all the marinade ingredients into a bowl, stir well and pour over the chicken, turn to coat, cover and marinate in the fridge overnight.

The next day, preheat a barbecue or grill.

Thread the chicken onto the soaked bamboo skewers, zig-zagging the meat back and forth as you go. Cook on the barbecue or under the grill for 3–4 minutes on each side until charred and tender. Leave to cool slightly before serving.

serves
4

M

500 g skinless chicken breast fillets

Marinade

250 ml natural yoghurt

2 tablespoons olive oil

2 garlic cloves, crushed

grated zest and juice of 1 unwaxed lemon

1–2 teaspoons chilli powder

1 tablespoon chopped fresh coriander

salt and black pepper

12 bamboo skewers, soaked in cold water for 30 minutes

super-easy *lamb* skewers

Dinner doesn't get much easier than this, but served with Rosemary Potatoes from page 46 and a simple side of fresh chopped tomatoes, you have a lovely Italian-style meal for four with minimum effort. The lamb is best done on a griddle pan.

Push the pieces of lamb onto the skewers until you run out of lamb (leave 6 cm clear at each end of the skewers). Season the lamb with salt.

Heat the griddle pan until quite hot. Lay the skewers on the pan and cook for about 10 minutes, until the lamb is cooked through and dark brown. Turn them over once halfway through cooking. You will need to cook them in batches.

Serve with a tomato salad and some Rosemary Potatoes, if liked.

serves
4

Q

M

500 g lamb fillet, cut into bite-sized chunks

salt

tomato salad, to serve

Rosemary Potatoes (page 46), to serve (optional)

12 bamboo skewers, soaked in cold water for 30 minutes

a ridged griddle pan

1 tablespoon olive oil

1 tablespoon lemon juice

12 small dried bay leaves

1 small unwaxed lemon, halved and cut into 12 small wedges

300 g skinless turkey breast fillets, cut into 12 large bite-sized chunks

salt and black pepper

Potato, olive and tomato salad

400 g new potatoes, scrubbed

12 stoned black olives, quartered

2 vine-ripened tomatoes, deseeded and cut into chunks

3 tablespoons chopped fresh flat leaf parsley

a handful of fresh basil leaves

1½ tablespoons lemon juice

1½ tablespoons olive oil

4 bamboo skewers, soaked in cold water for 30 minutes

turkey and *bay* skewers with potato, olive and tomato salad

serves
2

M

Turkey makes a nice alternative to chicken. It's cheap, easy to cook and very low in fat so it is a healthy choice, too. These turkey kebabs are infused with the tangy flavour of lemon and bay leaves.

Preheat the grill and line a grill pan with aluminium foil.

To make the potato, olive and tomato salad, cook the potatoes in boiling water for 12 minutes, or until tender. Drain and leave to cool slightly. Halve or quarter the potatoes if large, then put in a salad bowl with the olives, tomatoes, parsley and basil leaves. Mix together the lemon juice and olive oil and pour over the salad. Season with salt and pepper to taste and toss until everything is combined.

To make the kebabs, mix together the olive oil and lemon juice.

To assemble the skewers, follow this order of ingredients for each one: bay leaf, lemon, turkey, lemon, turkey, bay leaf, lemon, turkey, bay leaf.

Arrange the 4 skewers on the grill pan. Brush with the olive oil and lemon juice mixture and grill for 4 minutes. Turn the skewers, brush with more of the olive oil and lemon juice and grill for another 3–5 minutes, or until the turkey is cooked through.

Serve the turkey skewers with the potato, olive and tomato salad.

pepperoni, red pepper and *crouton* frittata

A frittata is Italy's version of an open omelette and it is one of the most convenient ways to use up leftover bits and bobs in the fridge. This one is packed with tasty chargrilled peppers and pepperoni, and must be served immediately, otherwise it goes on cooking and loses its soft creaminess. It can also be left to cool, cut into wedges and enjoyed as part of a lunch-on-the-go the following day.

serves
2

Q

M

4 eggs, lightly beaten

25 g Gruyère cheese, grated

1 spring onion, thinly sliced

25 g butter

50 g firm white bread, torn into small pieces

1 garlic clove, crushed

25 g jarred or fresh chargrilled red peppers, cut into strips

25 g sliced pepperoni

salt and black pepper

a medium-sized, ovenproof frying pan

Break the eggs into a bowl and beat well using a fork. Season well with salt and pepper and add half the cheese and spring onion. Mix well.

Melt half the butter in the ovenproof frying pan. Add the bread pieces and toss them for 2–3 minutes over high heat until golden brown and crispy. Remove from the heat and set aside.

Preheat the grill.

Add the remaining butter and the garlic to the pan, and when the butter starts to froth, add the beaten eggs. Turn the heat down and leave the eggs to cook gently for a few minutes. Arrange the pepperoni and red peppers on the top and sprinkle with the remaining cheese and reserved croutons.

Put the frying pan under the grill and cook for a further 2–3 minutes until the frittatta is puffed and just set but still wobbly. Remove from the grill and serve immediately with a crisp green salad or a tomato and basil salad.

Variation Also delicious made with any combination of the following: crumbled firm goats' cheese, sliced mushrooms, baby spinach leaves, courgettes or sliced cooked potatoes.

2 teaspoons coriander seeds

1 teaspoon cumin seeds

2 tablespoons olive oil

1 onion, finely chopped

2 garlic cloves, crushed

1 teaspoon ground cinnamon

¼–½ teaspoon cayenne pepper

300 g minced lamb

a pinch of salt

2 tablespoons chopped
fresh coriander

4 pita breads

a few salad leaves

natural yoghurt

1 tablespoon sesame seeds,
toasted in a dry frying pan

lamb in pita bread

Say goodbye to greasy late-night kebab horrors and hello to this fresh, fast and fantastic alternative. You'll never look back.

Put the coriander and cumin seeds into a small frying pan without oil and fry until they start to brown and release their aroma. Leave to cool slightly, then grind to powder with a pestle and mortar.

Heat the oil in a frying pan, add the onion, garlic and ground spices and fry gently for 5 minutes until softened but not golden. Increase the heat, add the lamb and the pinch of salt and stir-fry for 5–8 minutes until well browned. Stir in the fresh coriander.

Meanwhile, lightly toast the pita bread and cut a long slit in the side of each one. Carefully fill with a few salad leaves, add the minced lamb mixture, a spoonful of yoghurt and sprinkle with sesame seeds. Serve hot.

250 g sausages

1 onion, finely chopped

2 garlic cloves, crushed

2 ripe tomatoes, deseeded
and finely chopped

6 tablespoons olive oil

150 g frozen peas, defrosted

4 small flour tortillas

3 tablespoons mascarpone

1 small egg, beaten

salt and black pepper

a pastry brush

pea, sausage and *onion* calzone

In fact, this is a cheat's calzone — made with tortillas, filled and folded over to look like calzone. Lighter and quicker to make.

Cut away the skins of the sausages and pull the sausagemeat into chunks. Heat 3 tablespoons of the olive oil in a saucepan and fry the onion and garlic over gentle heat for 3–4 minutes, until the onion is starting to soften. Add the sausagemeat, season with salt and pepper and cook for 1–2 minutes longer, until golden. Add the tomatoes and peas and cook for 15 minutes or so, until all the liquid has disappeared and the meat is cooked.

Spoon one-quarter of the mixture onto one side of each tortilla, leaving a 2-cm border around the edges. Dot little bits of mascarpone over the sausagemeat mixture. Brush some beaten egg around the edge of the tortillas with a pastry brush. Fold over each tortilla to make a semi-circle. Press the edges down to seal them. Heat the remaining oil in a large frying pan over medium heat and fry the tortillas for 3–4 minutes on each side, until golden. Drain on kitchen paper and serve.

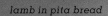
lamb in pita bread

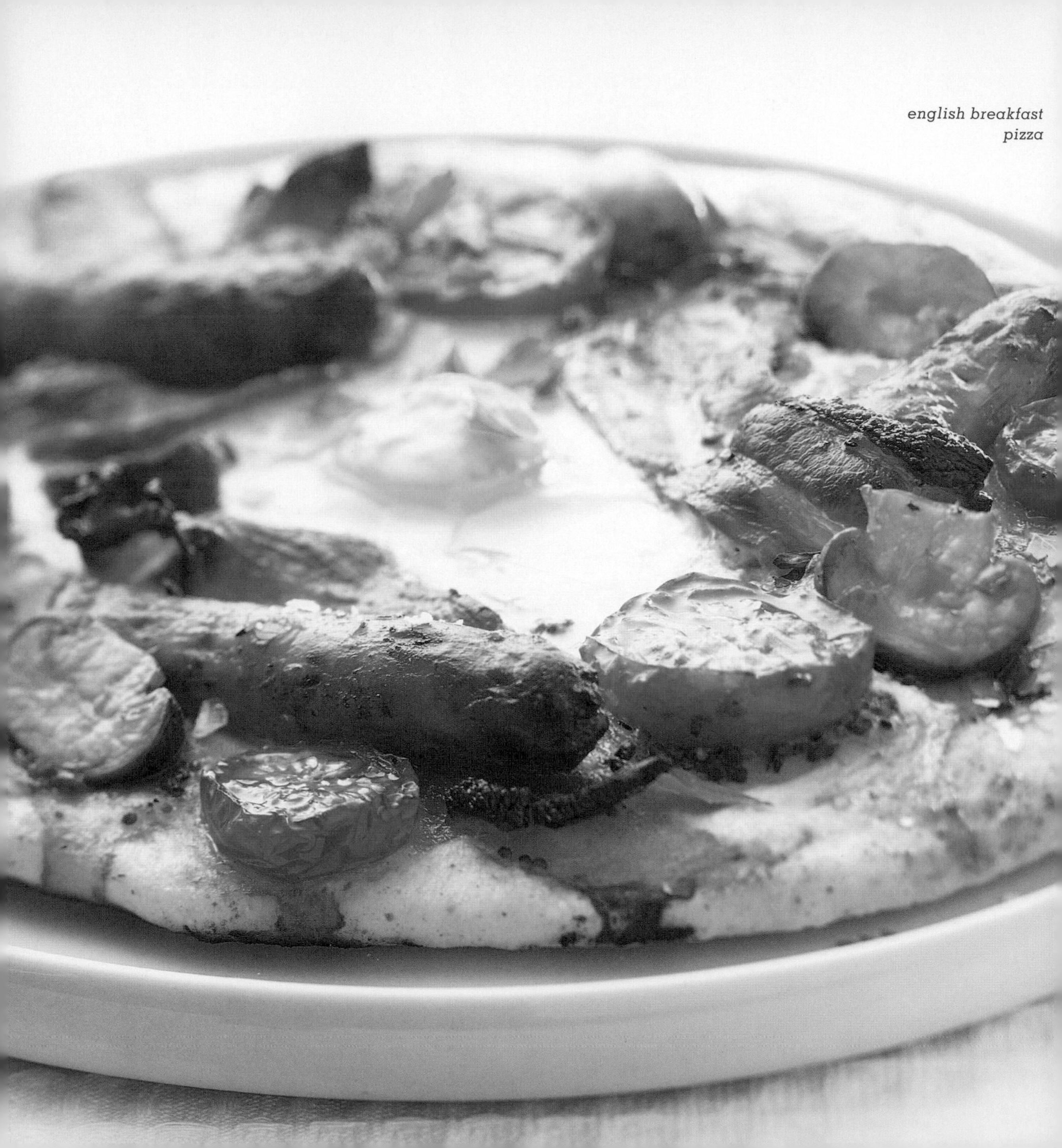

english breakfast pizza

english breakfast pizza

Breakfast on a pizza! The portions are hearty, so make sure you have worked up a really good appetite before you start.

serves
2

M

Put the baking trays in the oven and preheat the oven to 200°C (400°F) Gas 6.

Spread the mustard and ketchup over each pizza base. Arrange the tomatoes, sausages, bacon and mushrooms on each pizza, leaving a space in the middle for the egg.

Drizzle with a little oil and carefully transfer to the hot baking trays. Bake in the preheated oven for 15 minutes, then remove from the oven and increase the temperature to 220°C (425°F) Gas 7.

Crack an egg into the middle of each pizza and sprinkle with salt and pepper. Return the pizzas to the oven and cook for a further 5–10 minutes, until the egg is just set and the base is crisp and golden. Serve at once.

2 teaspoons wholegrain mustard

2 teaspoons tomato ketchup

2 x 20-cm ready-made deep pan pizza bases

5 small tomatoes, halved crossways

6 pork chipolata sausages

6 rashers of smoked streaky bacon

5 mushrooms, halved

2 eggs

1 tablespoon olive oil

salt and black pepper

2 baking trays

quattro stagioni pizza

The pizza for those who just can't make up their minds which one they want. You get all the best bits at once with this one.

serves
2–4

M

Put the baking tray in the oven and preheat the oven to 200°C (400°F) Gas 6.

Heat 2 tablespoons of the oil in a frying pan and cook the shallot for 2 minutes. Add the mushrooms and cook for a further 2–3 minutes, until softened and golden. Add salt and pepper to taste.

Brush the pizza base with a little oil. Spoon over the tomato sauce.

Pile the mushrooms over one quarter of the pizza. Arrange the ham and olives on another quarter and the artichoke hearts on the third section of pizza. Lay the mozzarella on the remaining section and put the anchovies on top.

Drizzle a little more oil over the whole pizza and sprinkle with salt and plenty of pepper. Carefully transfer to the hot baking tray and bake in the preheated oven for 20–25 minutes, until crisp and golden. Serve at once.

4 tablespoons olive oil

1 shallot, thinly sliced

150 g mushrooms, sliced

30-cm ready-made deep pan pizza base

Roasted Tomato Sauce (page 125) or shop-bought tomato sauce

50 g Parma ham, shredded

6 stoned black olives

4 artichoke hearts in brine or oil, drained and quartered

75 g mozzarella, sliced

4 anchovy fillets in oil, drained

salt and black pepper

a baking tray

tomato, caper and *anchovy* pizza

2 x 30-cm ready-made
pizza bases (not deep pan)

2 large, ripe tomatoes,
chopped

2 tablespoons capers,
rinsed and drained

12 anchovy fillets in oil,
drained and chopped

250 g mozzarella, chopped

a few fresh basil leaves

salt and black pepper

2 baking trays

Sometimes less is more, as with this pizza topping. If you have
the option, use the conventional rather than fan setting on your
oven to make sure you get a good, crisp base on the pizza.

Put the baking trays in the oven and preheat the oven to 200°C (400°F) Gas 6.

Divide the tomatoes, capers, anchovies, mozzarella and basil leaves
between the two pizza bases. Season with salt and pepper. Carefully
transfer the pizzas to the hot baking trays and bake in the preheated
oven for 10–12 minutes until bubbling and golden. Serve at once.

pepperoni pizza

30-cm ready-made
deep pan pizza base

2 tablespoons olive oil

Roasted Tomato Sauce
(page 125) or shop-bought
tomato sauce

1 large tomato, sliced

1 small red onion, sliced
and separated into rings

150 g mozzarella, drained
and sliced

100 g sliced pepperoni

salt and black pepper

a baking tray

Red onion, pepperoni and melted cheese on a deep pan base –
perfect Friday night comfort food.

Put the baking tray in the oven and preheat the oven to 200°C (400°F) Gas 6.

Put the pizza base on the baking tray. Brush with 1 tablespoon of the oil and
spoon over the tomato sauce.

Arrange the tomato slices over the sauce. Lay the onion rings on top, splash
over the remaining oil and sprinkle with salt and plenty of pepper. Bake in
the preheated oven for 20 minutes.

Remove from the oven and arrange the mozzarella and pepperoni slices
over the top. Return to the oven and cook for a further 10–15 minutes, until
risen and golden. Serve at once.

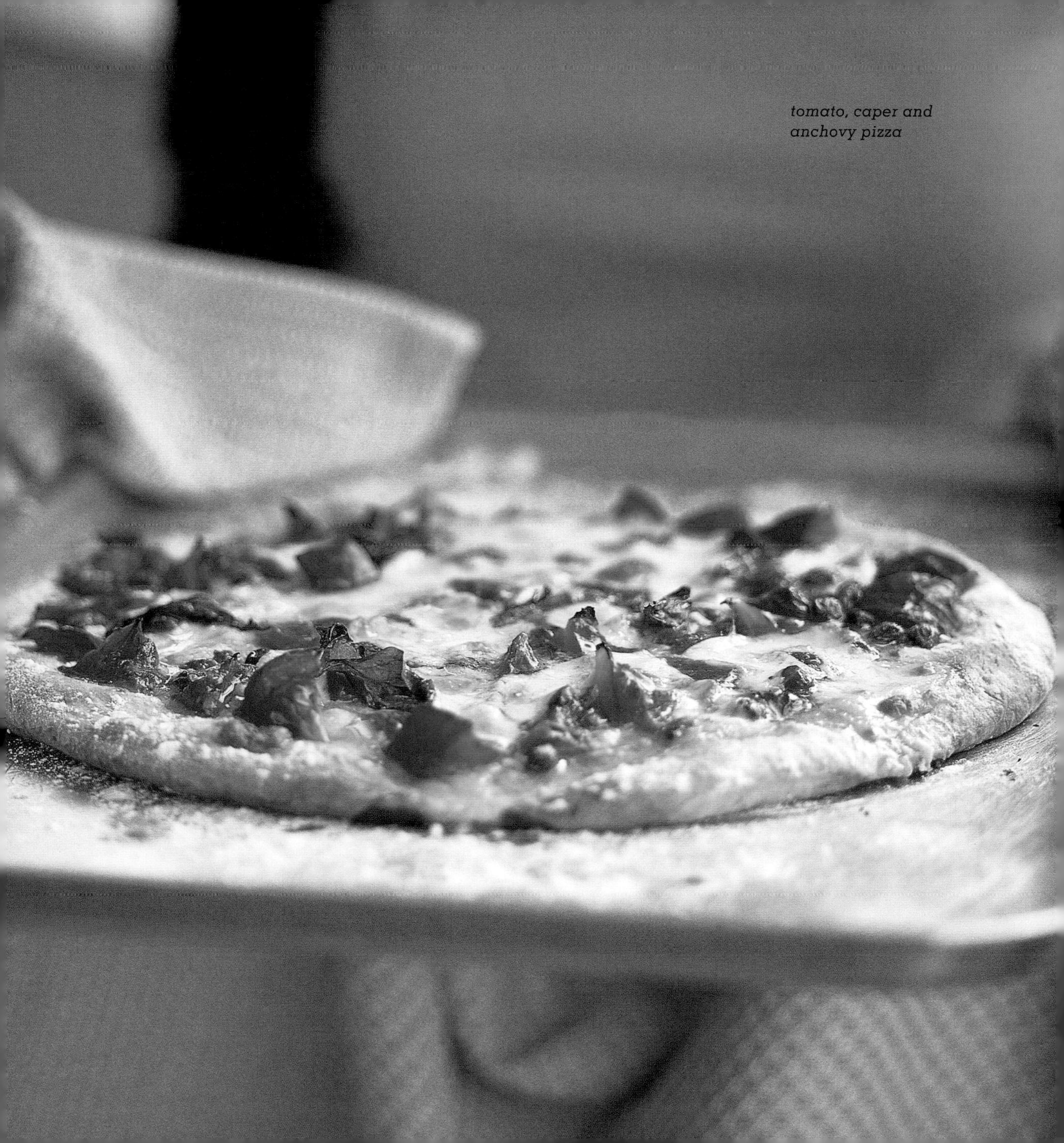

tomato, caper and anchovy pizza

prawn fried rice

prawn fried rice

This spicy Chinese-style rice dish is packed with flavour and a great way to use up leftover basmati rice after curry night. You could also use cooked prawns but add them after the egg.

serves **4**

Q

F

Heat the oil in a large frying pan and swirl to coat. Add the garlic, ginger and chilli and stir-fry for 30 seconds. Add the prawns, peas, spring onions and dried shrimp and fry for 2 minutes until the prawns turn pink.

Using a spatula, push the mixture to one side, add the eggs and scramble until set. Then add the rice and stir over a high heat for 2 minutes until heated through.

Stir in the soy sauce, lemon juice and coriander and serve.

Note Packets of dried shrimp are available in Chinese or South-east Asian stores. They keep very well, even after opening.

2 tablespoons sunflower oil

2 garlic cloves, crushed

3 cm fresh ginger, peeled and grated

1 red chilli, deseeded and chopped

350 g uncooked prawns, peeled, deveined and coarsely chopped

250 g frozen peas, defrosted

6 spring onions, chopped

4 tablespoons Asian dried shrimp (see Note)

2 eggs, lightly beaten

800 g cooked jasmine rice

3 tablespoons light soy sauce

juice of ½ lemon

2 tablespoons chopped fresh coriander

foil-baked *salmon* and *couscous*

Once you've put all the ingredients in the foil bag (which seals in all the flavours, making everything taste truly delicious) and popped it in the oven, there's nothing to do until 20 minutes later when it's ready to eat.

serves **2**

F

Preheat oven to 180°C (350°F) Gas 4.

Mix the couscous, courgette, carrots, peas and sweetcorn together in a bowl.

Fold a large sheet of aluminium foil or baking parchment in half and tightly fold one open side to seal. Holding the open 'bag' in one hand, carefully tip in the couscous mixture. Cut the lemon in half and squeeze the juice from one half into the stock. Cut the remaining half into slices.

Lay the salmon on top of the couscous and top with the lemon slices. Tightly fold over another open side of the bag, then carefully pour in the stock. Fold the remaining open side tightly. Bake in the preheated oven for 20–25 minutes, until the fish is cooked and couscous is fluffy.

150 g couscous

2 courgettes, thinly sliced

2 carrots, finely chopped

1½ tablespoons frozen peas

1½ tablespoons sweetcorn

1 unwaxed lemon

450 ml hot vegetable stock

3 salmon fillets

500 g dried pasta, such as tagliatelle, conchiglie or farfalle

salt and black pepper

Tomato salad

4 firm tomatoes

3 tablespoons olive oil

1½ tablespoons chopped fresh mint or parsley

Sauce

olive oil, for cooking

2 onions, finely sliced

1 teaspoon crushed coriander seeds

320 g tinned tuna in oil, lightly drained

1½ tablespoons capers (optional)

grated zest of 1 unwaxed lemon

125 ml milk

a handful of fresh mint sprigs, to serve

tuna, coriander and *lemon* pasta with tomato salad

serves
4–6

F

This is a delicious lunch or supper dish made with ingredients that, although not all strictly from the storecupboard, are to be found in most kitchens.

To make the tomato salad, peel the tomatoes using the instructions on page 10. Deseed the tomatoes, remove the cores and cut the flesh into small cubes. Add the oil, mint, salt and pepper to taste and set aside to develop the flavours.

Meanwhile, cook the pasta in plenty of boiling salted water, following the manufacturer's instructions, until al dente.

To make the sauce, cover the base of a frying pan with olive oil, add the onions and coriander seeds and cook slowly over medium heat. When the onions start to soften, add 3 tablespoons water and cover with a lid. Continue cooking over low heat until soft. This will take 15 minutes – do not rush (add extra water if necessary).

When the onions are very soft, add the tuna, capers, if using, lemon zest, lots of pepper and half the milk. Stir well, cover again and cook for 10 minutes over low heat (add the remaining milk if necessary).

Add the sauce and the tomato salad to the freshly cooked pasta and mix well. Sprinkle with mint sprigs and serve at once.

Variation You can simply use 300 g cherry tomatoes, cut in half, instead of the tomato salad.

fish cakes

fish cakes

These fish cakes freeze well, so are useful if you want to get ahead with meals for the week. Any type of fish can be used.

Cook the potatoes in boiling water for 20 minutes, Drain, return to the pan and shake over low heat to dry off. Mash the potatoes, add the butter and milk and mix well.

Preheat the oven to 180°C (350°F) Gas 4.

Put the fish into the prepared dish, cover with aluminium foil and bake for 10 minutes. Set aside to cool, then flake the fish into the potato. Beat one egg and add to the mixture, followed by the parsley, salt and pepper. Mix well.

Put the flour, breadcrumbs and remaining eggs in 3 separate bowls. Whisk the eggs. Divide the fish mixture into 8 equal pieces and shape into patties. Dust each fish cake with flour, then use one hand to dip them into the egg; use the other hand to coat in the breadcrumbs. Try to get an even coating.

Heat the oil and fry the fish cakes on each side for 5 minutes, until golden. Serve with mayonnaise.

serves 4

F

800 g potatoes, peeled

50 g butter

50 ml milk

400 g salmon, cod or halibut, skinned

3 eggs

a bunch of fresh parsley, chopped

100 g plain flour, plus extra for dusting

200 g breadcrumbs

300 ml olive oil

salt and black pepper

a shallow ovenproof dish, lightly greased

vegetable, seed and nut cakes

A delicious alternative to fish cakes, especially if you have vegetarians in the house, but even non-veggies will tuck into these. It's a great way to use up leftover mashed potato.

Mix the mashed potato with the spinach in a bowl. Heat 1 tablespoon of the oil in a frying pan, gently sauté the mushrooms and garlic for 5 minutes, then add to the potato mixture. Add the courgette and season with salt and pepper, then stir well. Divide into 8 equal pieces and roll into balls.

Mix the seeds and nuts together on a large plate and roll the balls in the mixture to coat well. Gently flatten them into patties. Heat the remaining oil in a frying pan and cook the patties on each side until golden, about 3–4 minutes.

serves 4

Q

F

500 g mashed potato

200 g cooked spinach

300 ml olive oil

100 g mushrooms, chopped

1 garlic clove, crushed

1 courgette, grated

100 g pumpkin seeds

40 g sesame seeds

100 g peanuts, chopped

salt and black pepper

bang bang *chicken*

serves
4

Q

M

400 g ready-cooked boneless chicken, such as smoked chicken, cold roast chicken or cold turkey

1 large carrot, peeled

salad leaves such as crispy iceberg lettuce or Chinese leaves, about 75 g

1 cucumber, cut into matchsticks

Bang bang dressing

5 tablespoons crunchy peanut butter

1 spring onion, thinly sliced

1 teaspoon sesame oil

1 teaspoon light soy sauce

1 teaspoon caster sugar

1 teaspoon Chinese white rice vinegar or cider vinegar

3 tablespoons hot water

This is a fantastic salad that's quite unusual and makes a more filling supper than your average leafy green salad – ready-cooked smoked or 'plain-roast' chicken is arranged on sticks of cucumber then topped with a creamy peanut butter dressing.

Remove any skin from the chicken and discard. Pull or cut the chicken into shreds the size of your little finger, then put onto a plate.

Make carrot ribbons by 'peeling' the carrot with a vegetable peeler to make ultra-thin long strips of carrot.

Tear any large salad leaves into bite-sized pieces. Arrange the leaves on a serving dish. Scatter the cucumber sticks and carrot ribbons over the leaves. Lastly, arrange the chicken on the top.

To make the bang bang dressing, put the peanut butter in a small bowl with the spring onion. Add the sesame oil, soy sauce, sugar, vinegar, 1 teaspoon cold water and the hot water to the bowl. Stir gently until well mixed. Taste the dressing – it should be a harmonious balance of salty, sweet and sour flavours, so add more vinegar, sugar or soy as you think is needed. The dressing should be just thin enough to spoon over the chicken, so if it is too thick stir in another tablespoon or so of hot water.

When the sauce seems perfect, spoon it over the chicken and serve.

new potato, crisp salami and sesame salad

This is miles away from the kind of potato salad you buy in a plastic tub. It's really easy to prepare but packed with flavour and can be eaten on its own or, if you leave out the salami, as a side dish with Beefburgers (page 184) or Fish Cakes (page 97). It also makes a good lunchbox filler.

To make the lemon mayonnaise, put the mayonnaise and lemon juice in a small bowl and stir well. Add a little salt and pepper.

If necessary, cut the potatoes into even-sized pieces. Put in a large saucepan. Cover with cold water, add a teaspoon of salt, bring to the boil, then simmer until tender. Drain and set aside.

Heat a frying pan to medium heat, add the sesame seeds and toast for about 6–8 minutes, stirring until golden. Set aside.

Reheat the frying pan until hot, add the salami slices and cook for a few minutes on each side until browned. Remove and drain on kitchen paper. (It will crisp up more as it cools.)

Arrange the rocket in a serving bowl. Toss the potatoes with the lemon mayonnaise and pile on top of the rocket. Scatter with half the toasted sesame seeds and dill. Crumble over the crisp salami and scatter with the remaining sesame seeds and dill to serve.

serves
6

M

800 g waxy new potatoes

2 tablespoons sesame seeds

150 g thinly sliced salami (a fatty, unflavoured variety)

75 g rocket

a small bunch of fresh dill, chopped

salt and black pepper

Lemon mayonnaise

3 tablespoons mayonnaise

½ tablespoon lemon juice

toad-in-the-*hole*

serves
4–6

M

115 g plain flour

2 large eggs

250 ml milk

a small bunch of fresh chives, snipped into 3-cm pieces with kitchen scissors

12 tiny chipolata sausages or cocktail sausages, or 6 larger sausages cut in half

4 tablespoons vegetable oil

salt and black pepper

a large baking tray or roasting tin

2 x 6-hole muffin tins

Imagine yourself back at home, sitting at the dinner table with a plate of Mum's toad-in-the-hole in front of you. Now you can recreate this taste of home with your own super-easy toad-in-the-holes. They're the ideal choice for feeding famished friends.

Preheat the oven to 220°C (425°F) Gas 7.

Adjust the oven shelves – you will be using the middle one for the muffin tin, so make sure there is plenty of room for the batter to rise above the tin. Put a shelf under the middle one and put a large tray or roasting tin on it to catch any drips.

To make the batter, put the flour, salt and pepper in a large bowl. Make a hollow in the centre, then break the eggs into the hollow. Pour the milk into the hollow. Using a wire whisk, mix the eggs with the milk. Start to mix the flour into the hollow. When all the flour has been mixed in, whisk the batter well to get rid of any lumps.

Add the snipped chives and whisk them into the batter. (The batter can be made up to 3 hours before you start cooking.)

Put 1 teaspoon oil into each hole of the muffin tin, then put it into the preheated oven to heat up. Remove the tin after 5 minutes – be careful, the oil will be very, very hot – and carefully put 1 chipolata or half a large sausage in each hole, then return to the oven for 5 minutes.

Pour or ladle the batter into a large jug and stir it once or twice.

Carefully remove the hot muffin tin as before, then stand back (the oil can splutter) and carefully pour the batter into each hole so each one is half full. Gently replace the tin in the oven and bake for 20 minutes until golden brown and crispy.

Remove from the oven and ease each toad out of its hole with a round-bladed knife. Eat straightaway with salad or green vegetables or even baked beans.

toad-in-the-hole

meatloaf

meatloaf

This is very easy and tasty. It goes really well with ketchup and the Rosemary Potatoes on page 46.

Put the loaf tin on a sheet of greaseproof paper and draw around the base. Cut out the rectangle and lay it in the bottom of the tin to line it.

Preheat the oven to 180°C (350°F) Gas 4.

Put the onion, garlic, egg, minced beef, oregano and Parmesan in a large bowl. Season well with salt and pepper.

Mix the ingredients with your fingers until everything is well combined. Spoon the mixture into the loaf tin and smooth the top with the back of a spoon. Transfer the tin to the preheated oven and cook for 45 minutes.

Remove the tin from the oven and turn the meatloaf out onto a chopping board. Cut in slices and serve with Rosemary Potatoes.

serves
4

M

1 onion, finely chopped

2 garlic cloves, crushed

1 egg, lightly beaten with a fork

900 g lean minced beef

2 teaspoons dried oregano

150 g grated Parmesan

salt and black pepper

a 450-g loaf tin

moussaka-filled
aubergines

moussaka-filled *aubergines*

A healthy version of the Greek holiday favourite, this looks smart but it's surprisingly fuss-free and guaranteed to please.

Preheat the grill.

Cut both aubergines in half lengthways and scoop out the flesh with a spoon, leaving a shell approximately 5 mm thick. Cut the aubergine flesh into small dice and set aside for the filling. Rub the oil into the aubergine shells and season the flesh lightly, then put under the grill for 5–6 minutes until golden brown and slightly softened. Transfer to the baking tray.

Preheat the oven to 200°C (400°F) Gas 6.

Put the lamb, onion and garlic in a non-stick frying pan and dry-fry over high heat for 5 minutes. Mix in the aubergine flesh, cinnamon, mint, tomato purée and 6 tablespoons of cold water, season with salt and pepper and cook for 5 minutes. Spoon the lamb filling into the aubergine shells. Mix the yoghurt with the egg yolk, nutmeg and seasoning, then pour this over the filling. Top with the sliced tomatoes and bake in the preheated oven for 20 minutes.

2 aubergines

1 teaspoon olive oil

300 g minced lamb

1 onion, finely chopped

2 garlic cloves, crushed

1 teaspoon ground cinnamon

1 teaspoon dried mint

1 tablespoon tomato purée

Topping

150 g Greek yoghurt

1 egg yolk

freshly grated nutmeg

2 tomatoes, sliced

a baking tray

pork with *sweet potato* mash

Pure comfort food! For a delicately spiced mash, stir in a teaspoon of ground cumin and half a teaspoon of chilli flakes, if liked. Serve the pork with your favourite green vegetable.

Mix together 1 tablespoon of the oil and the paprika and brush the mixture over the pork. Season with salt and pepper to taste.

Cook the sweet potatoes in boiling salted water until tender. Drain, then return the potatoes to the pan. Add the butter and remaining oil and mash the potatoes until smooth and creamy. Stir in the chopped coriander and season with salt and pepper to taste.

Heat the griddle pan until very hot. Griddle the pork for 5–6 minutes or until cooked right through. Turn halfway and brush with more oil, if necessary.

Divide the mash between 2 plates, then top with the pork.

1½ tablespoons olive oil, plus extra if needed

⅛ teaspoon paprika

2 pork loin fillets, 150 g each

salt and black pepper

Sweet potato mash

500 g sweet potatoes, peeled and cut into chunks

10 g butter

4 tablespoons chopped fresh coriander

a ridged griddle pan

vegetarian mains

pasta and bean soup

pasta and *bean* soup

This hearty soup of pasta and beans is a classic from the region of Puglia in Italy. Beans, pasta and potato all contribute to making it extra tasty and satisfying.

Heat the oil in a large saucepan, add the onion, garlic and potato and cook for 3–4 minutes until golden. Add the tomatoes and cook for 2–3 minutes until softened.

Add the stock, herbs, beans, pasta, chilli flakes, salt and pepper. Bring to the boil, then simmer for about 10 minutes, until the pasta and potatoes are cooked.

Ladle into bowls and serve sprinkled with a little Parmesan.

2 tablespoons olive oil

1 small onion, finely chopped

2 garlic cloves, crushed

1 potato, diced

2 ripe tomatoes, chopped

1.25 litres hot vegetable stock

a sprig of fresh thyme

2 x 400-g tins cannellini beans, drained

150 g dried pasta, such as orecchiette

a pinch of dried chilli flakes

salt and black pepper

grated Parmesan, to serve

summer *minestrone*

A very light, fragrant version of a soup that can sometimes be rather heavy. It has added taste thanks to the last-minute addition of pesto.

Bring a large saucepan of water to the boil. Add a good pinch of salt, then the pasta, and cook until al dente, or according to the manufacturer's instructions. Drain well.

Meanwhile, heat the oil in another large saucepan, add the onion and garlic and cook gently for 3 minutes. Add the celery and carrots and cook for a further 2 minutes. Add the tomatoes and cook for 2 minutes.

Add the stock and beans, bring to the boil, then simmer for 5–10 minutes, until the vegetables are cooked and tender.

Add the drained pasta, stir in the pesto and add salt and pepper to taste. Ladle into bowls, sprinkle with Parmesan and serve.

50 g small dried pasta shapes, such as stellete

1 tablespoon olive oil

1 red onion, chopped

1 garlic clove, crushed

2 celery stalks, thinly sliced

150 g carrots, thinly sliced

2 tomatoes, chopped

1.25 litres hot vegetable stock

150 g runner or green beans, thinly sliced

2 tablespoons pesto

salt and black pepper

1 tablespoon grated Parmesan, to serve

puy lentil and vegetable soup

serves
4–6

V

Puy lentils, which are grown in France, are very fashionable but they are also great at thickening soups without turning sludgy. They are a useful ingredient to have in your kitchen cupboard and a particularly popular, filling side dish for vegetarians.

Melt the butter in a large casserole dish or heavy-based saucepan. Add the carrots, leeks, onion and garlic and a large pinch of salt. Stir until everything is coated in butter and cook over medium heat, with the lid on, for 15 minutes, stirring occasionally.

Once the vegetables have softened, add the chilli flakes, oregano, tomatoes, lentils and stock. Cover again and leave to simmer for 30 minutes, or until the lentils are cooked. Season with salt and pepper to taste.

Transfer to bowls and serve with buttered toast and grated pecorino or Parmesan on the side.

50 g butter

2 carrots, finely chopped

2 leeks, white part only, thinly sliced

1 large onion, finely chopped

3 garlic cloves, sliced

½ teaspoon dried chilli flakes

2 teaspoons dried oregano

400-g tin chopped tomatoes

200 g Puy lentils

1 litre hot vegetable stock

salt and black pepper

grated pecorino or Parmesan, to serve

crusty bread, toasted and buttered, to serve

courgette, broad bean and lemon broth

serves
4

V

To make this broth more substantial, you can add a scoop of risotto rice at the same time as the broad beans and a little more stock to compensate. Frozen broad beans are a godsend and can be added to soups, risottos, pasta and lots more besides.

Heat the olive oil in a large saucepan. Peel the zest from the lemon in one large piece so it's easy to find later and add that to the pan. Add the onion, parsley and courgettes, cover and cook over low heat, stirring occasionally, for 8 minutes or until softening.

Remove the lemon zest. Add the broad beans and stock, season well with salt and pepper and return to the heat for a further 20 minutes.

Transfer a quarter of the soup to a blender, if you have one, and liquidize until smooth, then stir back into the soup. Skip this step if you don't have a blender. Check the seasoning and add lemon juice to taste.

Ladle the soup into bowls and serve with a fresh grinding of pepper.

2 tablespoons olive oil

1 unwaxed lemon

1 onion, chopped

3 tablespoons chopped fresh flat leaf parsley

500 g courgettes, sliced

300 g frozen broad beans

800 ml hot vegetable stock

salt and black pepper

*puy lentil and
vegetable soup*

*kitchen garden
soup*

kitchen garden soup

An old-fashioned nourishing soup, full of healthy green things. If you can't find sorrel in your supermarket, leave it out.

serves
4–6

V

Put the bay leaf in a large saucepan of water and bring to the boil. Add the cabbage quarters and blanch for 3 minutes. Drain the cabbage, pat dry and slice it thinly.

Heat the butter in a large saucepan. Add the cabbage, leeks, onion and 2 teaspoons salt and cook until softened, 5–10 minutes. Add the potatoes, parsley and 2 litres water. Add salt and pepper to taste and simmer gently for 40 minutes.

Stir in the peas, lettuce and sorrel and cook for 10 minutes more. Taste for seasoning. Ladle into bowls, add 1 tablespoon of butter to each and serve.

1 dried bay leaf

1 small cabbage, quartered

60 g butter, plus extra to serve

2 leeks, halved and sliced

1 onion, chopped

250 g new potatoes, chopped

a handful of fresh flat leaf parsley, chopped

250 g frozen peas

1 Little Gem lettuce, quartered and sliced thinly

a bunch of fresh sorrel, sliced

salt and black pepper

creamy *tomato* and *bread* soup

This is one of the most comforting soups on earth and has its origins in Italian peasant thrift. Leftover bread is never thrown away in Tuscany – here, it thickens a rich tomato soup, which is in turn enriched with Parmesan.

serves
6

V

Heat the stock slowly in a large saucepan. Meanwhile, heat the oil in a second large saucepan, add the onion and tomatoes and fry over gentle heat for about 10 minutes until soft. Push the mixture through a sieve and stir into the hot broth. Add the bread and garlic.

Cover and simmer gently for about 45 minutes until thick and creamy, whisking from time to time to break up the bread. Take care, because this soup can catch on the bottom.

To finish, stir the Parmesan into the soup, then add salt and pepper to taste. Ladle into bowls and trickle 2 tablespoons olive oil over each serving. Serve hot, warm or cold (but never chilled), with more Parmesan separately.

1.5 litres hot vegetable stock

4 tablespoons olive oil, plus extra to drizzle

1 onion, chopped

1.25 kg very ripe, soft tomatoes, roughly chopped

300 g stale white bread, thinly sliced, crusts removed (or breadcrumbs)

3 garlic cloves, crushed

125 g grated Parmesan, plus extra to serve

salt and black pepper

minestrone

serves
6–8

V

250 g smoked bacon, cut into strips (optional)

2 garlic cloves, crushed

2 large stalks of fresh parsley, lightly crushed

1 tablespoon olive oil

1 large onion, chopped

2 large potatoes, cubed and rinsed

3 carrots, cubed

2 celery stalks, sliced

3 tomatoes, halved, deseeded and chopped

200 g risotto rice

1 small round cabbage, quartered, cored and sliced

400-g tin cannellini beans, drained and rinsed

250 g frozen peas

3 small courgettes, halved lengthways, halved again into quarters, then thickly sliced

salt and black pepper

a handful of fresh basil, torn, to serve

crusty bread, to serve

grated Parmesan, to serve

There are as many versions of minestrone (big soup) as there are regions of Italy – and Italian grandmothers. Tomatoes, garlic, oil and pasta are used in southern recipes, beans in soups from central Italy, and rice in the north. In Genoa they add a spoonful of pesto, in Tuscany the soup is poured over their chunky unsalted bread, and in other areas, pork in various forms is added. Leave out the bacon for a veggie soup.

Put the bacon, if using, garlic and parsley in a large saucepan, heat gently and fry for 5–7 minutes. Add the olive oil, heat briefly, then add the onion and cook gently until softened but not browned.

Add the potatoes, carrots, celery, tomatoes, salt and pepper. Add 3 litres water and heat until simmering. Cook over low heat for about 20 minutes.

Add the rice and simmer for 10 minutes. Add the cabbage, bring to the boil and cook for 5 minutes, then add the cannellini beans, peas and courgettes. Cook for another 2–3 minutes until all the vegetables are tender.

Remove and discard the parsley stalks, add salt and pepper to taste, then serve sprinkled with torn basil. Crusty bread and grated Parmesan are the perfect accompaniments.

Note Remember that tinned beans often have sugar and salt added, so keep that in mind when you season the finished soup.

minty *pea risotto* soup

This is a cross between a soup and a risotto and should be soupy in consistency. It's a good option when your kitchen is a bit of a barren wasteland – you're bound to have a bag of peas in the freezer and the other ingredients are easy to buy. There is, in fact, pancetta in here, but do just leave it out if you're vegetarian. It will taste just as fabulous.

serves
4–6

V

30 g butter

1 onion, finely chopped

150 g pancetta, cubed (optional)

400 g frozen peas, defrosted

2 tablespoons olive oil, plus extra for drizzling

150 g risotto rice

1.5 litres hot vegetable stock, plus extra if necessary

2 tablespoons fresh mint, shredded

salt and black pepper

grated Parmesan, to serve

Melt the butter in a medium saucepan, then add the onion and pancetta, if using. Cook over low/medium heat, with the lid on, for 8 minutes, or until the onion is softened and translucent. Stir occasionally.

Meanwhile, put half the peas in a food processor with the olive oil and blend until puréed. If you don't have a food processor, roughly mash the peas with the oil in a bowl using a fork.

Add the rice to the softening onion and stir until well coated in butter. Pour in the stock and add the puréed peas. Simmer, uncovered, for 15 minutes.

Add the remaining peas, season with salt and pepper and cook for a further 8–10 minutes, or until the rice is tender. Stir in the mint and add a little more stock if you think it needs to be soupier.

Transfer to bowls, drizzle with olive oil and grind over some pepper. Serve with grated Parmesan.

garlic and *chilli* rice soup

This is a substantial soup – really more of a light stew. Boiled rice soups are popular in many Asian countries, especially China where they are called congees. The spring greens work very nicely with the simple Asian flavours here.

1 tablespoon vegetable oil

2 teaspoons sesame oil

2 garlic cloves, crushed

4 spring onions, finely chopped

2 teaspoons finely grated fresh ginger

1 small red chilli, deseeded and thinly sliced

100 g long grain white rice

1.5 litres hot vegetable stock

1 tablespoon soy sauce

a bunch of spring greens, roughly shredded

a small bunch of fresh coriander, chopped

white pepper

Put the oils in a saucepan and set over high heat. Add the garlic and spring onions and cook until the garlic is turning golden and just starting to burn. This will give the soup a lovely, nutty garlic flavour. Add the ginger, chilli and rice to the pan and stir-fry in the garlic-infused oil for 1 minute. Add the stock and soy sauce and bring to the boil.

Cover with a lid and cook over low heat for 30 minutes, until the rice is soft and the soup has thickened. Add the spring greens and cook for 5 minutes, until they turn emerald green and are tender. Ladle the soup into bowls, sprinkle the coriander over the top and season to taste with white pepper.

miso soup with *ramen noodles* and stir-fried *vegetables*

Japanese broths are generally made with a base of stock and soy sauce or miso. Miso (soya bean paste) is probably the most essential Japanese food and easily found in the Asian foods aisle at your supermarket. It will keep for ages in the fridge.

3 tablespoons red miso paste

1 tablespoon soy sauce

½ teaspoon sugar

1.25 litres hot vegetable stock

200 g ramen or thin egg noodles

1 tablespoon olive oil

2 teaspoons sesame oil

2 teaspoons finely sliced fresh ginger

2 shallots, thinly sliced

2 leeks, very finely chopped

200 g Savoy cabbage leaves, finely shredded

200 g red cabbage, finely shredded

Combine the miso, soy sauce, sugar and stock in a large saucepan set over medium heat and warm until the miso has completely dissolved. Keep warm over low heat. Cook the noodles according to the manufacturer's instructions. Drain well and divide between 4 bowls.

Put the oils in a large frying pan over high heat. Add the ginger and shallots and cook for just a few seconds to flavour the oil. Add the leeks and cabbage and stir-fry for 2 minutes, until the vegetables are crisp and glistening with oil.

Ladle the warm miso mixture over the noodles and top with the stir-fried vegetables. Serve immediately.

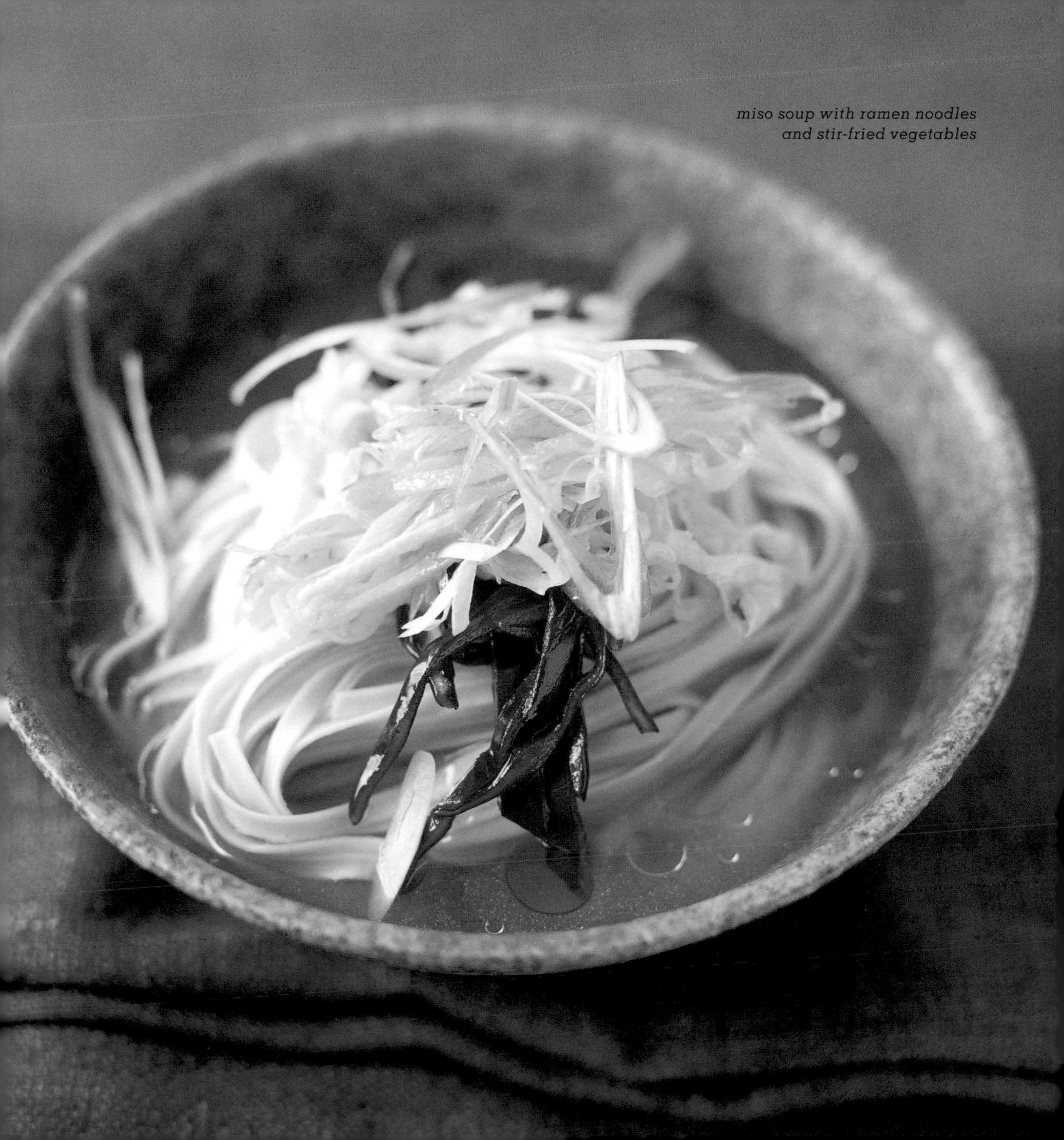

miso soup with ramen noodles and stir-fried vegetables

spaghetti with *garlic, olive oil* and *chilli* sauce

350 g dried pasta, such as spaghetti or linguine

grated Parmesan (optional), to serve

Garlic, olive oil and chilli dressing

150 ml olive oil

4 garlic cloves, peeled but whole

1 small to medium dried chilli (to taste), finely chopped

2 handfuls of fresh parsley, finely chopped

serves 4–6

Q

V

If you like spicy and ridiculously simple food, this is for you. Make this dressing swiftly, cook the pasta al dente, use the best-quality ingredients and serve straightaway. Apart from the fresh parsley, you only need things you are likely to have lurking in your kitchen cupboards already. If not, buy them and know that you will always have the means to make this fantastic pasta dish, no matter how empty your fridge is.

Bring a large saucepan of water to the boil. Add a good pinch of salt, then the pasta, and cook until al dente, or according to the manufacturer's instructions.

While the pasta is boiling, slowly heat the olive oil in a frying pan with the garlic and chilli. When the garlic turns golden, discard it. Drain the pasta, then return it to the saucepan. Add the hot flavoured oil, chilli pieces and chopped parsley and stir well. Serve at once, with Parmesan, if using.

Variation For spice lovers, arrabbiata is a tomato-based version of the recipe above. The word arrabbiata means 'rabid' and is used in Italian to mean 'angry'. It is a popular dish in Rome and generally made on demand in simple eateries. To make a simplified arrabbiata, use the Roasted Tomato Sauce recipe on page 125, but double the amount of garlic and dried chilli flakes and replace the basil with parsley.

spaghetti with garlic,
olive oil and chilli sauce

penne with broccoli
and pine nut pesto

penne with *broccoli* and *pine nut* pesto

This can be rustled up in a matter of minutes. All you need is fresh broccoli and a few basic ingredients and you have the makings of a fine TV dinner.

Bring a large saucepan of water to the boil. Add a good pinch of salt, then the pasta, and cook until al dente, or according to the manufacturer's instructions. Cook the broccoli in a separate saucepan of boiling, salted water for 10–12 minutes until very soft.

Meanwhile, heat a dry frying pan until hot, add the pine nuts and cook, turning them frequently, until golden and toasted. Set aside.

Heat the olive oil in a small saucepan and add the garlic and chilli. Gently cook for 2–3 minutes until softened. Remove from the heat and set aside.

Drain the broccoli, return it to the pan and mash coarsely with a fork.

Drain the pasta and return it to the warm pan. Add the mashed broccoli, garlic and chilli oil and toasted pine nuts. Mix well, squeeze in a little lemon juice and add salt and pepper to taste. Top with Parmesan shavings.

serves
2

Q

V

175 g dried pasta, such as penne or fusilli

175 g broccoli, cut into florets

2 tablespoons pine nuts

3 tablespoons olive oil

3 garlic cloves, crushed

1 red chilli, deseeded and finely chopped

½ a lemon

Parmesan shavings, to serve

salt and black pepper

vegetarian mains   121

pasta with roasted aubergine and tomato

pasta with *roasted* *aubergine* and *tomato*

A vegetarian pasta with the beefy substance of aubergine. It needs time in the oven, so you can get on with something else.

serves
4

V

2 aubergines,
cut into 3-cm cubes

500 g ripe tomatoes, quartered

2 garlic cloves, halved

4 tablespoons olive oil

300 g dried pasta, such as
fusilli or penne

1 shallot, finely chopped

2 tablespoons chopped
fresh mint

2 tablespoons chopped
fresh coriander

juice of 1 lime

salt and black pepper

Preheat the oven to 200°C (400°F) Gas 6.

Put the aubergine, tomatoes and garlic into a large roasting tin. Add 2 tablespoons of the oil and mix. Sprinkle with salt and pepper and cook in the preheated oven for 30–40 minutes, turning the vegetables from time to time, until the aubergine is tender and golden.

Meanwhile, bring a large saucepan of water to the boil. Add a good pinch of salt, then the pasta, and cook until al dente, or according to the manufacturer's instructions.

Drain the pasta well and return it to the warm pan. Add the roasted aubergine and tomatoes, then the shallot, mint, coriander and lime juice Add the remaining oil and toss well to mix.

three-cheese baked penne

A simplified version of that old-time favourite, macaroni cheese, but with no flour and no risk of lumps.

serves
4

V

350 g dried pasta,
such as penne or macaroni

400 g mascarpone

2 tablespoons
wholegrain mustard

300 g Fontina cheese, grated

4 tablespoons grated
Parmesan

salt and black pepper

a baking dish

Bring a large saucepan of water to the boil. Add a good pinch of salt, then the pasta, and cook until al dente, or according to the manufacturer's instructions. Meanwhile, preheat the oven to 200°C (400°F) Gas 6.

Drain the pasta well and return it to the warm pan. Add the mascarpone and stir to mix. Add the mustard, Fontina and Parmesan, with salt and pepper to taste. Stir to mix.

Transfer to the baking dish and cook in the preheated oven for 25–30 minutes until golden and bubbling.

pasta with *ricotta, cherry tomatoes* and *basil*

3 tablespoons salt

500 g dried pasta, such as farfalle, fusilli or penne

1 punnet ripe cherry tomatoes

about 250 g ricotta, drained

5 tablespoons olive oil

a large handful of fresh basil leaves, sliced

grated Parmesan, to serve

salt and black pepper

serves
4–6

Q

V

You could almost call this a salad, but it's not; it's pasta with an uncooked sauce. It is just the thing when temperatures soar, because it is light but still substantial.

Bring a large saucepan of water to the boil. Add a good pinch of salt, then the pasta, and cook until al dente, or according to the manufacturer's instructions.

Meanwhile, halve or quarter the tomatoes, depending on their size. Put in a large, shallow bowl and crumble in the ricotta. Add the oil, basil and about ½ teaspoon salt. Mix well and set aside.

When the pasta is cooked, drain well, then add to the bowl with the tomatoes, 2–3 tablespoons grated Parmesan and some pepper. Toss well. Add more salt and/or Parmesan to taste. Serve warm or at room temperature, with extra Parmesan and pepper.

noodle mountain

300 g dried egg noodles

6 tablespoons vegetable oil

4 garlic cloves, crushed

12 cm fresh ginger, peeled and finely chopped

4 onions, finely sliced

4 chillies, finely chopped

1 Chinese cabbage, finely shredded

250 g beansprouts

200 ml soy sauce

juice of 4 limes

2 bunches of spring onions, chopped

400 g cashew nuts, chopped

serves
10

Q

V

Throwing a party? Need something quick, stress-free and vegetarian-friendly? Here's your answer – a noodle mountain to feed at least 10 people. Other vegetables can always be added, such as asparagus, baby corn, thin green beans, carrots, mushrooms or water chestnuts.

Cook the noodles according to the manufacturer's instructions, drain and transfer to a bowl of cold water until needed.

Heat the oil in a large frying pan and add the garlic, ginger, onions and chillies. Cook over medium heat for 5 minutes until softened. Add the cabbage and beansprouts and stir briefly. Drain the noodles well and add to the pan. Toss with 2 large spoons, then add the soy sauce, lime juice, spring onions and cashew nuts. Mix well and serve.

*pasta with ricotta,
cherry tomatoes and basil*

roasted tomato sauce

roasted tomato sauce

This is the ultimate tomato sauce – the tomatoes are roasted first to give them a really sweet flavour. Master this and you'll be serving it with spaghetti, as part of vegetable lasagne, or as a pizza topping, as well as having a base for soups or stews.

serves
4

V

Preheat the oven to 230°C (450°F) Gas 8.

Put the tomatoes, olive oil, garlic, lemon zest, chilli flakes and seasoning in a roasting tin in a single layer. Toss well. Roast for 45 minutes, or until the tomatoes are browned and the juices reduced to a glaze.

Transfer the tomatoes and all the pan juices to a deep bowl, add the basil and, using a stick blender, purée until smooth. Season to taste. Serve hot with some freshly cooked pasta or leave to cool in a plastic container.

Note During the summer months, when tomatoes are plentiful and at their best, make up several quantities of this sauce and freeze for use in the winter.

1 kg vine-ripened tomatoes, roughly chopped

2 tablespoons olive oil

2 garlic cloves, crushed

grated zest of
1 unwaxed lemon

a pinch of dried chilli flakes

2 tablespoons chopped fresh basil

salt and black pepper

a roasting tin

vegetable noodle stir-fry

4 tablespoons vegetable oil

1 garlic clove, crushed

5 cm fresh ginger,
peeled and finely chopped

1 onion, thinly sliced

1 chilli, finely chopped

125 g egg noodles

2 pak-choi, roughly chopped

1 leek, cut into strips

75 g beansprouts, trimmed

75 g mushrooms, sliced

3 tablespoons soy sauce

juice of 1 lime

a bunch of fresh coriander,
chopped

serves
4

Q

V

When making this dish, prepare the ingredients in advance, so the stir-fry can be quickly put together. You can vary the vegetables but always use the onion, garlic, ginger and chilli.

Heat the oil in a large frying pan. Add the garlic, ginger, onion and chilli and cook over medium heat, stirring constantly.

Bring a large saucepan of water to the boil. Add the noodles and cook according to the manufacturer's instructions. Drain thoroughly.

Add the pak-choi, leek, beansprouts and mushrooms to the frying pan and stir-fry for 2–3 minutes.

Add the soy sauce, lime juice and noodles and use 2 spoons to mix the vegetables and noodles together. Top with the chopped coriander and serve immediately.

roast peppers stuffed with pasta

4 yellow or red peppers

50 g very fine spaghetti,
broken into pieces

6 tablespoons olive oil

12 ripe cherry tomatoes,
quartered

2 garlic cloves, crushed

3 tablespoons chopped
fresh basil

50 g pine nuts, chopped

½ teaspoon dried chilli flakes
(optional)

75 g grated pecorino or
Parmesan

salt and black pepper

a baking dish, lightly greased

serves
4

V

These peppers are a vegetable and pasta course in one. They should be luscious and soft, with a wrinkled, browned exterior. The garlicky cherry tomatoes help to keep the pasta moist.

Slice the tops off the peppers and reserve. Scrape out and discard all the seeds and white pith. Set the peppers upright in the baking dish small enough to fit them snugly. If they don't stand upright, shave a little piece off the base, but not right through.

Bring a saucepan of water to the boil. Add a good pinch of salt, then the pasta, and cook until al dente, or according to the manufacturer's instructions. Drain well and toss with 2 tablespoons of the olive oil. Meanwhile, preheat the oven to 220°C (425°F) Gas 7.

Put the tomatoes in a bowl with another 2 tablespoons of oil, the garlic, basil, pine nuts, chilli flakes and pecorino and mix well. Add the pasta to the peppers, filling them by two-thirds, then spoon in the tomato mixture. Put the pepper lids on top and brush all over with the remaining olive oil. Bake in the preheated oven for 25–30 minutes or until the peppers start to wrinkle.

*roast peppers
stuffed with pasta*

pea and *parmesan* risotto

Making a risotto is simple, but it takes time and risotto rice needs constant stirring as it cooks. Look for risotto rice called arborio, carnaroli and vialone nano in the supermarket.

serves
4

V

2 tablespoons olive oil

1 onion, finely chopped

2 garlic cloves, crushed

300 g risotto rice

120 g frozen peas

about 750 ml hot vegetable stock

20 g butter

100 g grated Parmesan

salt and black pepper

chopped fresh flat leaf parsley, to serve

Heat the olive oil in a medium, heavy-based pan over very low heat and stir in the onion and garlic. Cook gently for about 10 minutes until the onion is translucent but not yet brown. Stir in the rice and make sure it is well coated in oil, then stir in the peas.

Turn up the heat to medium and add a ladle of the hot vegetable stock. Stir gently and as soon as the liquid is absorbed by the rice, add another ladle of stock.

Keep on stirring the rice gently and continuously so it doesn't stick to the the pan, and keep on adding the hot stock. It will take about 20 minutes of stirring before the rice is tender. Taste a few grains with a teaspoon. The mixture should be creamy and moist, but not dry or very wet and soupy – the exact amount of stock you will need depends on the brand of rice you use and how fast the rice is cooking.

As soon as the rice is tender, turn off the heat. Add the butter, salt and pepper to taste, plus half the Parmesan. Stir gently into the rice, then cover the pan and leave for 4–5 minutes.

Sprinkle the parsley on top, then serve with the remaining Parmesan.

butternut squash, sage and *chilli* risotto

about 1.5 litres hot
vegetable stock

125 g butter

1 large onion, finely chopped

1–2 fresh or dried red chillies,
deseeded and finely chopped

500 g butternut squash
or pumpkin (or swede),
peeled and finely diced

500 g risotto rice

3 tablespoons chopped
fresh sage

75 g grated Parmesan

salt and black pepper

serves
6

V

This tastes wonderful on its own – it's filling and delicious as a vegetarian main – but you could also serve it in smaller portions for meat-eaters as a side with grilled lamb chops. Buying fresh sage just for this dish may seem like an extravagance but in fact sage leaves freeze very well: wash and pat them dry, then pop them loose in a freezer bag and freeze for up to 1 year. Note that the flavour becomes even more intense when the leaves are frozen so use them in moderation.

Pour the stock into a saucepan and keep at a gentle simmer. Melt half the butter in a large, heavy saucepan and add the onion. Cook gently for 10 minutes until soft, golden and translucent but not browned. Stir in the chopped chillies and cook for 1 minute. Add the butternut squash, and cook, stirring constantly over the heat for 5 minutes, until it begins to soften slightly. Stir in the rice to coat with the butter and vegetables. Cook for a few minutes to toast the grains.

Begin adding the stock, a large ladle at a time, stirring gently until each ladle has almost been absorbed by the rice. The risotto should be kept at a bare simmer throughout cooking, so don't let the rice dry out – add more stock as necessary. Continue until the rice is tender and creamy, but the grains still firm and the squash beginning to disintegrate. (This should take 15–20 minutes depending on the type of rice used – check the manufacturer's instructions.)

Taste and season well with salt and pepper, then stir in the sage, remaining butter and all the Parmesan. Cover, leave to rest for a couple of minutes, then serve.

parmesan and
butter risotto

parmesan and *butter* risotto

Even if you have desperately bare kitchen cupboards and fridge, you're likely to have what's needed for this comforting risotto.

serves 4–6

V

about 1.5 litres hot vegetable stock

150 g butter

1 onion, finely chopped

500 g risotto rice

150 ml dry white wine

100 g grated Parmesan

salt and black pepper

Put the stock in a saucepan and keep at a gentle simmer. Melt half the butter in a large, heavy saucepan and add the onion. Cook gently for 10 minutes until soft, golden and translucent but not browned. Add the rice and stir until well coated with the butter and heated through. Pour in the wine and boil hard until it has reduced and almost disappeared. This will remove any raw alcohol taste.

Begin adding the stock, a large ladle at a time, stirring gently until each ladle has almost been absorbed by the rice. Don't let the rice dry out – add more stock as necessary. Continue until the rice is tender and creamy, but the grains still firm. (This should take 15–20 minutes depending on the type of rice used – check the manufacturer's instructions.) Taste and season well with salt and pepper, then stir in the remaining butter and all the Parmesan. Cover and leave to rest until the cheese has melted, then serve.

risotto primavera

This is a chance to use up fresh spring vegetables. The choice is yours but make sure they're are at their freshest and greenest.

serves 4

V

100 g butter

3 tablespoons olive oil

1 onion, diced

1 garlic clove, crushed

275 g risotto rice

about 1 litre hot vegetable stock

620 g mixed green vegetables, such as green beans, runner beans, broad beans, green cabbage, peas or spinach, all chopped into evenly-sized pieces

75 ml white wine

a bunch of fresh flat leaf parsley, chopped

125 g grated Parmesan

salt and black pepper

Heat the butter and olive oil in a large saucepan. Add the onion and garlic and cook over low heat for 5 minutes until softened and translucent. Add the rice, stirring with a wooden spoon to coat the grains thoroughly with butter and oil. Add a ladle of stock to the rice, mix well and leave to simmer. When the liquid has almost evaporated, add another ladle of stock and stir thoroughly until it bubbles away. Continue, stirring the risotto as often as possible and adding more stock as needed.

After the risotto has been cooking for 12 minutes, add all the vegetables and mix well. Add the remaining stock, white wine, salt and pepper. Cook, stirring, for a further 4–5 minutes, then mix in the chopped parsley and grated Parmesan.

courgette and tomato risotto

serves
4

V

This risotto is baked in the oven, which means you are not going to get the creamy texture of one cooked conventionally. However, the good thing is that it doesn't need constant stirring.

Preheat the oven to 200°C (400°F) Gas 6.

Put the oil in the casserole dish and set over low heat. Add the onion and garlic and fry gently for 2–3 minutes until the onion has softened. Add the rice and rosemary and cook for 1 minute before adding the courgettes. Stir for 1 minute, or until the rice becomes opaque, then add the tomatoes. Pour the hot stock into the casserole and stir well to combine all the ingredients. As soon as the liquid starts to simmer, cover with the lid and cook in the preheated oven for 30 minutes. Stir through the butter and half of the Parmesan, then sprinkle the remaining Parmesan on top to serve.

2 tablespoons olive oil

1 onion, chopped

1 garlic clove, crushed

330 g risotto rice

2 tablespoons fresh rosemary needles

2 courgettes, roughly chopped

2 tomatoes, chopped

750 ml hot vegetable stock

50 g butter

50 g grated Parmesan

a flameproof, lidded casserole dish

couscous with feta, dill and spring beans

serves
4

Q

V

Marinating the feta in this fresh-tasting salad lifts it from a salty, creamy cheese to something much more complex, so it's well worth it, even if it's just for 5 minutes.

Put the couscous in a large bowl and pour over the hot water. Cover with clingfilm or a plate and leave to swell for 10 minutes.

Pour the olive oil into a mixing bowl and add the garlic, shallots, dill, chives and lemon zest and flesh and lots of black pepper – the coarser the better. Add the feta, turn in the oil and set aside while you cook the beans.

Bring a medium saucepan of unsalted water to the boil. Add the sugar snap peas, bring back to the boil and cook for 1 minute. Add the broad beans, bring back to the boil and cook for 1 minute. Finally, add the peas and cook for 2 minutes. Drain.

Uncover the couscous, stir in the hot beans, transfer to bowls and top with the feta, spooning over the flavoured oil as you go. Stir well before serving.

275 g couscous

400 ml hot water

5 tablespoons olive oil

1 garlic clove, crushed

3 shallots, thinly sliced

2 tablespoons chopped fresh dill

2 tablespoons snipped fresh chives

1 tablespoon zest and flesh of fresh lemon, finely chopped

250 g feta cheese, chopped

150 g sugar snap peas

150 g frozen baby broad beans, defrosted

150 g frozen peas, defrosted

black pepper

couscous with feta,
dill and spring beans

moroccan-style
roasted vegetable couscous

Couscous is an excellent storecupboard staple for the busy cook as it doesn't need cooking – it is simply soaked in hot water or stock and fluffed up with a fork. It is classically served with a rich North African stew called a tagine, named after the dish with the conical lid, in which it is cooked. The couscous acts like an absorbent sponge and mops up the sauce. This roasted vegetable couscous is spicy and satisfying. If time is very short, look out for pre-packed, peeled and chopped vegetables from supermarkets but beware that they will be more expensive.

Preheat the oven to 200°C (400°F) Gas 6.

Remove the thin skin from the onions and slice them into thin wedges. Peel the sweet potato and cut into chunks. Core and deseed the peppers, then chop. Trim the leeks, then split them and wash well. Dry with kitchen paper and cut into large chunks.

Put the prepared vegetables and garlic on the baking tray or in the small roasting tin. Pour the olive oil over the top, add the chilli flakes and use your hands to toss the vegetables until they are coated with the oil mixture. Place the tray or tin in the preheated oven and cook for about 20–25 minutes, or until golden and tender.

Meanwhile, put the couscous in a large bowl and pour over the hot stock or water. Cover with clingfilm or a plate and leave to swell for 10 minutes.

Use a fork to fluff up the couscous, then add the roasted vegetables and mint sprigs. Add a little lemon juice and season with salt and pepper to taste. Serve immediately whilst still warm.

Variation Add 50 g crumbled or diced feta cheese to the couscous.

175 g red onions

175 g sweet potato

175 g red peppers

175 g leeks

2 garlic cloves, halved

2 tablespoons olive oil

½ teaspoon dried chilli flakes

150 g couscous

300 ml hot vegetable stock or water

a handful of fresh mint sprigs

lemon juice, to taste

salt and black pepper

a non-stick baking tray or small roasting tin

1 onion, finely chopped

1 garlic clove, crushed

400 ml hot vegetable stock

175 g bulghur wheat

2 teaspoons cumin seeds

1½ teaspoons ground coriander

a pinch of hot chilli powder

150 g carrots, diced

400-g tin chopped tomatoes

275 g courgettes, diced

200 g mushrooms, chopped

410-g tin chickpeas, drained and rinsed

200 g baby spinach

salt and black pepper

chickpea and *vegetable* bulghur pilau

serves
4

V

Serve this Indian-style pilau with a spoonful of natural yoghurt and some chopped fresh coriander.

Put the onion and garlic in a large saucepan with 4 tablespoons of the stock. Cover and cook over medium heat for 5 minutes until softened.

Stir in the bulghur wheat, spices and carrots and cook for 1–2 minutes, stirring, then add the tomatoes, courgettes, mushrooms, chickpeas and the remaining stock. Add the salt and some pepper. Bring to the boil, then reduce the heat, cover and simmer for 15 minutes.

Stir the pilau, pile the spinach on top, then replace the lid and cook for a further 5 minutes. Mix the cooked spinach into the pilau and serve.

4 large portobello or field mushrooms

olive oil (see method)

200 ml white wine

2 garlic cloves, crushed

juice of 1 lemon

3 tablespoons chopped fresh parsley

salt and black pepper

grilled portobello *mushrooms*

serves
4

Q

V

These whole, large mushrooms are just as good served alongside a meat main as they are as a vegetarian starter. They require barely any preparation, and are grilled, on your plate and covered in a simple sauce in a matter of minutes.

Preheat the grill.

Pull the stalks off the mushrooms and set the caps gill side up on an oiled grill pan. Chop the stalks finely and set aside. Brush the mushrooms with olive oil, season with salt and pepper and cook under the grill for 5 minutes.

Meanwhile, put 3 tablespoons olive oil in a frying pan with the white wine, garlic, lemon juice, parsley and the reserved chopped stalks. Bring to the boil, then boil hard to reduce by half. Season well and take off the heat. Transfer the mushrooms to plates and pour the sauce over the top.

*chickpea and
vegetable
bulghur pilau*

greek barley
salad

ratatouille

All the vegetables for ratatouille must be fresh and full of flavour in order to show off this famous French dish at its best.

serves
4

V

Heat the oil in a large saucepan. Add the onions and garlic and cook, stirring, for 3 minutes without browning.

Add the peppers, aubergines and courgettes to the pan and cook for 5 minutes, stirring frequently. Add the tinned tomatoes, oregano and marjoram. Season generously with salt and pepper and stir thoroughly. Bring the mixture to the boil, then reduce the heat under the pan and simmer for 25 minutes, stirring occasionally.

Transfer the ratatouille to a large serving bowl. Sprinkle with the chopped parsley or basil, then drizzle with some extra olive oil and serve.

Note Try making this the day before you plan to eat it. The flavour really seems to improve overnight and benefits from being cooled and reheated.

3 tablespoons olive oil, plus extra to serve

2 onions, chopped

2 garlic cloves, crushed

2 red peppers, deseeded and cut into chunks

2 aubergines, cut into chunks

3 courgettes, thickly sliced

2 x 400-g tins peeled chopped tomatoes

½ teaspoon dried oregano

½ teaspoon dried marjoram

a bunch of fresh flat leaf parsley or basil, chopped

salt and black pepper

greek *barley* salad

This hearty version of the traditional and much-loved salad incorporates satisfyingly chewy barley. If you are able to buy good-quality dried Greek oregano from speciality food stores, it will make all the difference to the flavour.

serves
4

V

Cook the barley in a saucepan of boiling salted water for 30 minutes or until tender. Drain and set aside until needed.

In a large serving bowl, whisk together the lemon juice and zest, vinegar and oil, then stir in the warm barley and mix well. Leave to cool.

Soak the onion in a bowl of iced water for 10 minutes. Drain well.

Add the drained onion to the barley along with the tomatoes, cucumber, green pepper and olives and mix to combine. Season to taste with salt and pepper.

Crumble the feta over the top of the salad and sprinkle with oregano.

100 g pearl barley

juice and finely grated zest of 1 unwaxed lemon

2 teaspoons white or red wine vinegar

4 tablespoons olive oil

1 red onion, thinly sliced

4 tomatoes, chopped

1 large cucumber or 2 small (Lebanese), deseeded and chopped

1 green pepper, deseeded and chopped

20 stoned black olives

150 g feta cheese

1 teaspoon dried oregano

salt and black pepper

1 red onion, sliced

1 red or yellow pepper,
deseeded and sliced

1 teaspoon sunflower oil

2 large mushrooms, sliced

1 garlic clove, crushed

3 teaspoons Cajun spice mix

2 tomatoes, chopped

410-g tin pinto beans,
drained and rinsed

juice of ½ unwaxed lime

4 soft wholemeal tortillas

4 tablespoons soured cream

100 g iceberg lettuce, shredded

salt and black pepper

bean burritos

serves 4

Q

V

This is a filling and spicy meal – good for throwing together
in super-quick time. Keep plenty of napkins handy!

Fry the onion and peppers in the sunflower oil for 3 minutes in a non-stick
frying pan. Add the mushrooms, garlic and 2 teaspoons of the Cajun spice
and stir-fry for 1 minute, then mix in the tomatoes, cover the pan and cook
for 2 minutes.

Meanwhile, roughly mash the beans together with the remaining Cajun
spice, the lime juice and seasoning to taste.

Spread each tortilla with 1 tablespoon of the soured cream. Spoon on
a quarter of the mashed beans and a quarter of the vegetable mixture.
Top with shredded lettuce and roll up to serve.

1 tablespoon butter

1 tablespoon sunflower oil

1 small onion, sliced

3 large eggs

40 g firm blue cheese such
as Roquefort, crumbled

salt and black pepper

*an 18-cm frying pan
(measure the base,
not the top)*

onion and *blue cheese* omelette

serves 1

Q

V

A strong blue cheese, such as Roquefort, adds a powerful flavour
to this omelette. However, if you prefer a more delicate flavour,
use creamy dolcelatte or Gorgonzola, chopped into small pieces.

Put half the butter and oil in the frying pan and heat until the butter has
melted. Add the onion and fry gently for about 10 minutes, until golden and
caramelized, stirring occasionally.

Meanwhile, break the eggs into a bowl and whisk briefly with a fork, just
enough to mix the yolks and whites. Season with salt and pepper. Using
a slotted spoon, add the onions to the eggs and mix gently.

Increase the heat to medium-high and add the remaining butter and oil.
When the pan is hot, pour in the omelette mixture. Using a spatula or the
back of a fork, draw the mixture from the sides to the centre as it sets.
Let the liquid flow and fill the space at the sides. Sprinkle the cheese over
the top, fold over a third of the omelette to the centre, then fold over the
remaining third. Serve immediately.

bean
burritos

minted courgette frittata

minted *courgette* frittata

This frittata (an Italian-style omelette) needs to be finished off under the grill so make sure your frying pan is ovenproof, and that the handle is away from the grill's direct heat.

Cook the potatoes in a saucepan of boiling, salted water until just tender. Drain thoroughly. Meanwhile, break the eggs into a bowl and whisk briefly with a fork. Season well with salt and pepper. Mix in the chopped mint.

Meanwhile, heat the oil in the frying pan, add the onion and cook gently for about 10 minutes, until soft and pale golden. Add the courgettes and stir over low heat for 3–4 minutes until just softened. Add the potatoes and mix gently.

Preheat the grill.

Pour the eggs over the vegetables and cook over low heat until the frittata is lightly browned underneath and has almost set on top. Slide under the grill for 30–60 seconds, to set the top. Serve, cut into wedges.

serves 3–4
Q
V

250 g baby new potatoes, thickly sliced

6 large eggs

2 tablespoons chopped fresh mint

2 tablespoons olive or sunflower oil

1 large onion, chopped

4 courgettes, sliced

salt and black pepper

a 24-cm frying pan (measure the base, not the top)

spiced *aubergine* dahl

'Dahl' literally means lentil and refers to any Indian dish of stewed, spiced lentils. This recipe uses yellow split lentils which require no soaking and cook quickly. It benefits from being made a day in advance, which gives the flavours time to mingle and mellow. Serve with steamed basmati rice or bread.

Heat the sunflower oil in a saucepan over high heat. Add the onions and stir-fry for 6–8 minutes, until they start to become golden. Reduce the heat and stir in the garlic, ginger, cumin seeds and curry powder. Stir-fry for 1–2 minutes, then add the lentils and 600 ml water. Bring to the boil, add the aubergine and cherry tomatoes and reduce the heat to low. Cover and simmer gently for 25–30 minutes, stirring occasionally, until the dahl is thick and the lentils are tender.

Season well with salt and stir in the coriander. Serve with steamed basmati rice or bread, if you like.

serves 2
V

3 tablespoons sunflower oil

2 onions, finely chopped

4 garlic cloves, crushed

1 teaspoon finely grated fresh ginger

1 tablespoon cumin seeds

2 tablespoons mild curry powder

175 g dried yellow split lentils

1 aubergine, cut into bite-sized pieces

8 cherry tomatoes

8 tablespoons chopped fresh coriander

salt

30-cm ready-made
deep pan pizza base

2 tablespoons olive oil

Roasted Tomato Sauce
(page 125) or shop-bought
tomato sauce

200 g small tomatoes,
quartered or sliced

150 g mozzarella, sliced

salt and black pepper

a handful of fresh basil
leaves, to serve

a baking tray

margherita pizza

serves
2–4

V

The red, white and green on this pizza symbolize the tricolore of the Italian flag. Since the topping is so simple, try to use the best ingredients you can afford.

Put the baking tray in the oven and preheat the oven to 200°C (400°F) Gas 6.

Brush the pizza base with half the oil. Spoon over the tomato sauce and arrange the tomatoes and mozzarella on top.

Drizzle the pizza with the remaining oil and sprinkle with salt and plenty of pepper. Carefully transfer to the hot baking tray and cook for 20–25 minutes, until crisp and golden.

Scatter the basil leaves over the hot pizza and serve.

---

2 red peppers

2 yellow peppers

2 garlic cloves, crushed

a small bunch of fresh flat
leaf parsley, finely chopped

3 tablespoons olive oil

Roasted Tomato Sauce
(page 125) or shop-bought
tomato sauce

150 g tomatoes, sliced
or halved

150 g mozzarella, sliced

salt and black pepper

a baking tray

a small roasting tin

roasted pepper pizza

serves
4

V

Roasting peppers is a lovely way to bring out their sweetness. Make sure they are still warm when you add the flesh to the oil, so that they absorb the flavours of the garlic and parsley.

Put the baking tray in the oven and preheat the oven to 220°C (425°F) Gas 7.

Put the peppers in the roasting tin and bake for 30 minutes, turning them occasionally, until the skin blisters and blackens.

Meanwhile, put the garlic and parsley in a bowl. Add 2 tablespoons of the olive oil and salt and pepper to taste.

Remove the peppers from the oven, cover with a clean tea towel and set aside for about 10 minutes, until cool enough to handle but still warm. Pierce the bottom of each pepper and squeeze the juice into the oil mixture. Skin and deseed the peppers. Cut the flesh into 2-cm strips and add to the mixture.

Brush the pizza base with the remaining olive oil. Spoon over the tomato sauce and arrange the tomatoes and mozzarella on top. Spoon the pepper mixture over the top. Carefully transfer to the hot baking tray and cook for 20–25 minutes, until crisp and golden.

*roasted
pepper
pizza*

food to impress

asparagus tagliatelle

Because asparagus is reasonably costly and is in season for such a short time, it really is a treat, so keep it simple. It is often served blanched with hollandaise sauce but this tagliatelle recipe is a perfect starter or light main course, combining the prime spears with a handful of other fresh, good-quality foods. There are very few ingredients needed so you can splash out to make sure they are the best.

Put the cream in a small saucepan and bring to the boil. Reduce the heat to a low simmer and cook for 8–10 minutes, until slightly thickened. Set aside.

Bring a large saucepan of water to the boil. Add a good pinch of salt, then the pasta, and cook according to the manufacturer's instructions. 2 minutes before the pasta is cooked, add the asparagus to the boiling water. Drain well and return to the warm pan with the reduced cream, lemon zest and juice, parsley and half of the Parmesan. Toss together, season well with salt and pepper and serve with the remaining Parmesan sprinkled on top.

Variation As a substitute to asparagus, fry 1 grated courgette in 1 tablespoon of butter over medium heat until softened and golden. Add the courgette to the well-drained pasta along with the other ingredients.

serves 4 / Q / V

250 ml single cream

300 g dried pasta, such as tagliatelle or pappardelle

1 bunch of fine asparagus, trimmed and each spear cut into 4

grated zest and juice of 1 unwaxed lemon

3 tablespoons chopped fresh flat leaf parsley

100 g grated Parmesan

salt and black pepper

creamy *smoked salmon* pasta

Smoked salmon is a bit of a luxury but a little goes a long way in this simple but quite grown-up pasta dish. Add the salmon at the last moment so it doesn't overcook or break into tiny pieces.

Bring a large saucepan of water to the boil. Add a pinch of salt, then the pasta, and cook until al dente, or according to the manufacturer's instructions.

Meanwhile, put the cream and garlic into a small saucepan. Add salt and pepper to taste and heat gently until warmed through.

Drain the pasta and return it to the warm pan. Add the cream, smoked salmon and Parmesan, toss gently, then divide between 4 bowls or plates. Sprinkle with chives and extra Parmesan and serve.

serves 4 / Q / F

300 g dried pasta, such as fusilli or farfalle

300 ml double cream

2 garlic cloves, crushed

200 g smoked salmon, cut into 1-cm strips

4 tablespoons grated Parmesan, plus extra to serve

salt and black pepper

2 tablespoons snipped fresh chives, to serve

baked *pasta* with *aubergine, basil* and *ricotta*

400 g dried pasta, such as rigatoni or penne

185 ml olive oil

1 aubergine, halved and very thinly sliced

1 onion, chopped

2 garlic cloves, crushed

3 tomatoes, chopped

a small bunch of fresh basil leaves, torn

125 ml red wine

125 g ricotta

45 g grated Parmesan or pecorino

salt and black pepper

an ovenproof dish

serves
4

V

This is sensible entertaining: spend a little time in the kitchen preparing the ingredients, then throw them all in a baking dish and let them do their thing in the oven for 20 minutes, leaving you free to chat, open a bottle of wine and relax. Cooking should not be stressful and this bake proves that it is possible. The sauce should be sweet and fruity so do use up any soft, over-ripe tomatoes. Ideally you should use a light olive oil here; extra virgin olive oil burns at a lower temperature and will make the aubergine bitter and oily.

Preheat the oven to 220°C (425°F) Gas 7.

Bring a large saucepan of water to the boil. Add a good pinch of salt, then the pasta, and cook until al dente, or according to the manufacturer's instructions. Drain well and return to the warm pan.

Heat the oil in a frying pan and when it is hot, but not smoking, cook the aubergine slices, in batches, for 2 minutes on each side, until golden. Remove and place on kitchen paper. Repeat to cook all of the aubergine. Pour off all but 1 tablespoon of oil from the frying pan, add the onion and garlic and cook for 2–3 minutes, stirring often. Add the tomatoes, basil and red wine, 250 ml water, salt and pepper to taste and bring to the boil. Boil for 10 minutes, until you have a thickened sauce. Stir in the aubergine, then add to the pasta and stir well.

Put the mixture in the ovenproof dish. Spoon the ricotta on top, sprinkle over the Parmesan and bake in the preheated oven for 20 minutes until golden and crispy around the edges.

pasta with *parma ham, rocket* and bubbling *blue cheese*

Do try to find the right cheese for this pasta – it needs to be cylindrical and have a firm rind so that you can slice it in rounds. That way it will keep its shape when it is grilled.

serves
4

Q

M

Bring a large saucepan of water to the boil. Add a good pinch of salt, then the pasta, and cook until al dente, or according to the manufacturer's instructions.

Preheat the grill.

Heat a little of the oil in a non-stick frying pan, add the Parma ham and cook for 1 minute on each side until crisp. Remove and drain on kitchen paper. Add the remaining oil to the pan. When hot, add the cherry tomatoes and cook for 3–4 minutes until split and softened.

Meanwhile, cut each cheese in half crossways, put cut side up under the grill and cook for 2–3 minutes, until golden and bubbling.

Break the Parma ham into pieces and add to the tomato pan. Add the Marsala, parsley and salt and pepper to taste.

Drain the pasta well and return it to the warm pan. Add the Parma ham and tomato mixture and toss gently to mix. Divide between 4 bowls or plates and sprinkle with rocket. Using a spatula, slide a bubbling cheese half on top of each serving. Grind over some pepper and serve.

300 g dried pasta, such as pappardelle or tagliatelle

2 tablespoons olive oil

8 slices of Parma ham

250 g cherry tomatoes

2 Bresse Bleu or mini Cambazola cheeses, 150 g each

2 tablespoons Marsala or sherry

2 tablespoons chopped fresh flat leaf parsley

a handful of rocket

salt and black pepper

rigatoni with *pork* and *lemon* ragu

2 tablespoons olive oil

400 g minced pork

1 onion, finely chopped

2 garlic cloves, crushed

4 anchovy fillets in oil, drained

2 tablespoons fresh rosemary needles

finely grated zest and juice of 1 unwaxed lemon

375 g dried pasta, such as rigatoni or penne

500 ml milk

75 g stoned green olives, chopped

75 ml double cream

a good grating of fresh nutmeg

4 tablespoons Parmesan shavings, plus extra to serve

salt and black pepper

serves
4

M

In Italy, pork is often braised with milk, as it tenderizes the meat and the juices mingle with the milk to provide a sweet, meaty sauce. Rosemary is lovely and robust with pork but you could use chopped sage – just add it earlier when you brown the pork so it frazzles a little.

Put a large saucepan of salted water on to boil for the pasta.

Meanwhile, heat the olive oil in a large frying pan over high heat and add the pork. Leave it for a few minutes until it browns, then turn it over and allow the other side to brown too. Add the onion, garlic, anchovies, rosemary and lemon zest and stir to combine with the pork. Reduce the heat, cover and leave the onion to soften for 10 minutes, stirring occasionally so the ingredients don't stick to the bottom of the pan.

When the salted water in the large pan is boiling, add the pasta and cook according to the manufacturer's instructions until al dente.

When the onion is translucent, add the milk, lemon juice and olives, and bring to the boil, uncovered, scraping the base of the pan to loosen any sticky bits and incorporating them into the sauce. Simmer for about 15–20 minutes, or until about two-thirds of the liquid has evaporated and the pork is soft. Stir in the cream, then season with salt, pepper and nutmeg.

Drain the rigatoni, put it back into its pan and spoon in the pork ragu. Add the Parmesan shavings, stir well and transfer to bowls. Sprinkle the extra Parmesan shavings on top.

500 g dried lasagne sheets

1 quantity sauce from
the Spaghetti Bolognese
recipe (page 67)

300 g mozzarella, diced

4 tablespoons grated
Parmesan

salt and black pepper

White sauce

1 litre milk

1 small garlic clove

50 g butter

50 g plain flour

*an ovenproof dish,
about 30 x 20 x 7 cm*

lasagne

serves
8

M

Lasagne, just like Mum makes. It's a bit fiddly and you'll need to be happy to spend some time in the kitchen, but just wait for the appreciative oohs and aahs round the table when you serve it up. Don't forget you need to have made the Bolognese sauce from the Spaghetti Bolognese recipe (page 67) first.

Preheat the oven to 190°C (375°F) Gas 5.

Bring a large saucepan of water to the boil. Add a pinch of salt, then the lasagne sheets, one at a time so that they don't stick together. Cook for 5 minutes, then drain and tip the lasagne into a bowl of cold water. Drain again and pat dry with kitchen paper.

To make the white sauce, put the milk and garlic into a small saucepan and heat gently until warm. Melt the butter in a separate saucepan, then stir in the flour and cook for 1 minute. Gradually add the warm milk, stirring constantly to make a smooth sauce. Bring to the boil, then simmer for 2–3 minutes. Remove and discard the garlic clove. Season with salt and pepper to taste.

Put 3–4 tablespoons of the Bolognese sauce into the ovenproof dish, spread evenly across the base of the dish and cover with a layer of lasagne. Spoon over some white sauce and a few pieces of mozzarella and continue adding layers, starting with another layer of Bolognese sauce and finishing with the white sauce and mozzarella, until all the ingredients have been used. Sprinkle with pepper and Parmesan, then bake in the preheated oven for 30 minutes until the top is crusty and golden.

lasagne   *carbonara*

carbonara

This is not for the health-conscious: lots of eggs, cream, butter, Parmesan and streaky bacon. It's perennially popular, and for good reason. Make it for a special dinner and serve it with a leafy green salad to temper the richness of the pasta.

serves
4–6

Q

M

Bring a large saucepan of water to the boil. Add a good pinch of salt, then the pasta, and cook until al dente, or according to the manufacturer's instructions. Meanwhile, put the eggs and egg yolks in a bowl and mix lightly with a fork. Add the butter, cream, grated Parmesan and lots of pepper. Leave to stand without mixing.

Chop the bacon into slivers. Cover the base of frying pan with olive oil and heat through. When the oil is hot, add the bacon. When the fat starts to run from the bacon, add the garlic and stir well. Continue frying until the bacon becomes crisp and golden. Add the bacon and pan juices to the freshly cooked pasta and mix vigorously. Beat the egg mixture lightly with a fork and pour over the pasta. Mix well and serve at once with extra Parmesan and plenty of pepper – the butter will melt and the eggs will cook in the heat of the pasta.

500 g dried pasta, such as penne or spaghetti

Carbonara sauce

2 whole eggs

5 egg yolks

25 g butter

125 ml single cream

6 tablespoons grated Parmesan, plus extra to serve

200 g streaky bacon

olive oil, for frying

1 garlic clove, crushed

black pepper

sesame *chicken* and *vegetable* noodle salad

This recipe is typical of many with an Asian influence in that most of the sauce ingredients are storecupboard basics. That said, balsamic vinegar has replaced traditional Chinese black vinegar, which can be tricky to find. Similarly, if you're lucky enough to have a Chinese grocery near you, you will probably be able to find garlic chives but don't worry if not – just use regular chives instead. Unfortunately, watercress does perish quite quickly so try gently wrapping the leftovers in a clean, damp tea towel. Stored like this in the fridge, it should stay fresh for a couple of days.

Preheat the oven to 180°C (350°F) Gas 4.

To make the sesame dressing, put the sesame oil, soy sauce, vinegar and sugar in a small bowl and stir for a few seconds until the sugar has dissolved. Set aside until needed.

Put the chicken in the roasting tin with 65 ml water, cover firmly with aluminium foil and cook in the preheated oven for 30 minutes. Remove from the oven and leave to cool. When cool enough to handle, shred the chicken and set aside.

Cook the noodles in boiling water for 3 minutes. Rinse them under cold water to cool and drain well. Heat the vegetable oil in a frying pan over high heat. Add the chives, leeks and red pepper and stir-fry for 1 minute, until the vegetables have just softened. Remove the pan from the heat and stir in the beansprouts and watercress.

To serve, put the chicken, noodles and vegetables in a large bowl. Add the dressing and sesame seeds and toss well.

serves
4

M

2 skinless chicken breast fillets

175 g thin egg noodles

2 tablespoons vegetable oil

2 handfuls of fresh garlic chives or regular chives, snipped into 3-cm lengths

1 leek, thinly sliced

1 small red pepper, deseeded and thinly sliced

100 g beansprouts

a small bunch of watercress, leaves picked

1 tablespoon sesame seeds, lightly toasted in a dry frying pan

Sesame dressing

2 tablespoons sesame oil

2 tablespoons light soy sauce

1 tablespoon balsamic vinegar

1 teaspoon caster sugar

a small roasting tin

vodka risotto with *lemon*

3 tablespoons olive oil

1 small onion, chopped

1 tender, inner celery stalk, chopped (optional)

3 garlic cloves, crushed

300 g risotto rice

about 1.25 litres hot vegetable stock

grated zest and juice of 1 unwaxed lemon

3 tablespoons vodka

2 tablespoons grated Parmesan, plus extra to serve

salt and black pepper

serves
4

V

Risotto is just the thing when friends drop in unexpectedly, and it's a very social dish to prepare if everyone helps with the stirring. It really only needs ingredients you're likely to have already, including vodka, a bottle of which is bound to be in the house somewhere. This recipe is light, so is especially good for impromptu late-night eating, but it is equally good as a side dish or starter since the flavours are subtle and go with most things. It can be made without celery, if you're improvising and have none, but everything else is mandatory.

Heat the oil in a large saucepan. Add the onion, celery (if using) and a pinch of salt. Cook over medium heat until soft, 2–3 minutes. Add the garlic and rice and continue cooking, stirring for about 1 minute, until the rice is well coated with oil.

Add a ladle of the stock and cook, stirring all the while, until the stock has been absorbed. Continue adding ladles of stock as the rice absorbs it. The rice is done when it is tender on the outside but still firm. Timing depends on the type and age of the rice, but 20–30 minutes is usual. Towards the end of cooking, add smaller ladles more often, rather than drowning the rice.

When the rice is cooked, stir in 1 tablespoon of the lemon zest, 2 tablespoons of the lemon juice, the vodka, Parmesan and some pepper. Mix and taste for salt and lemon. Serve immediately with extra Parmesan and pepper.

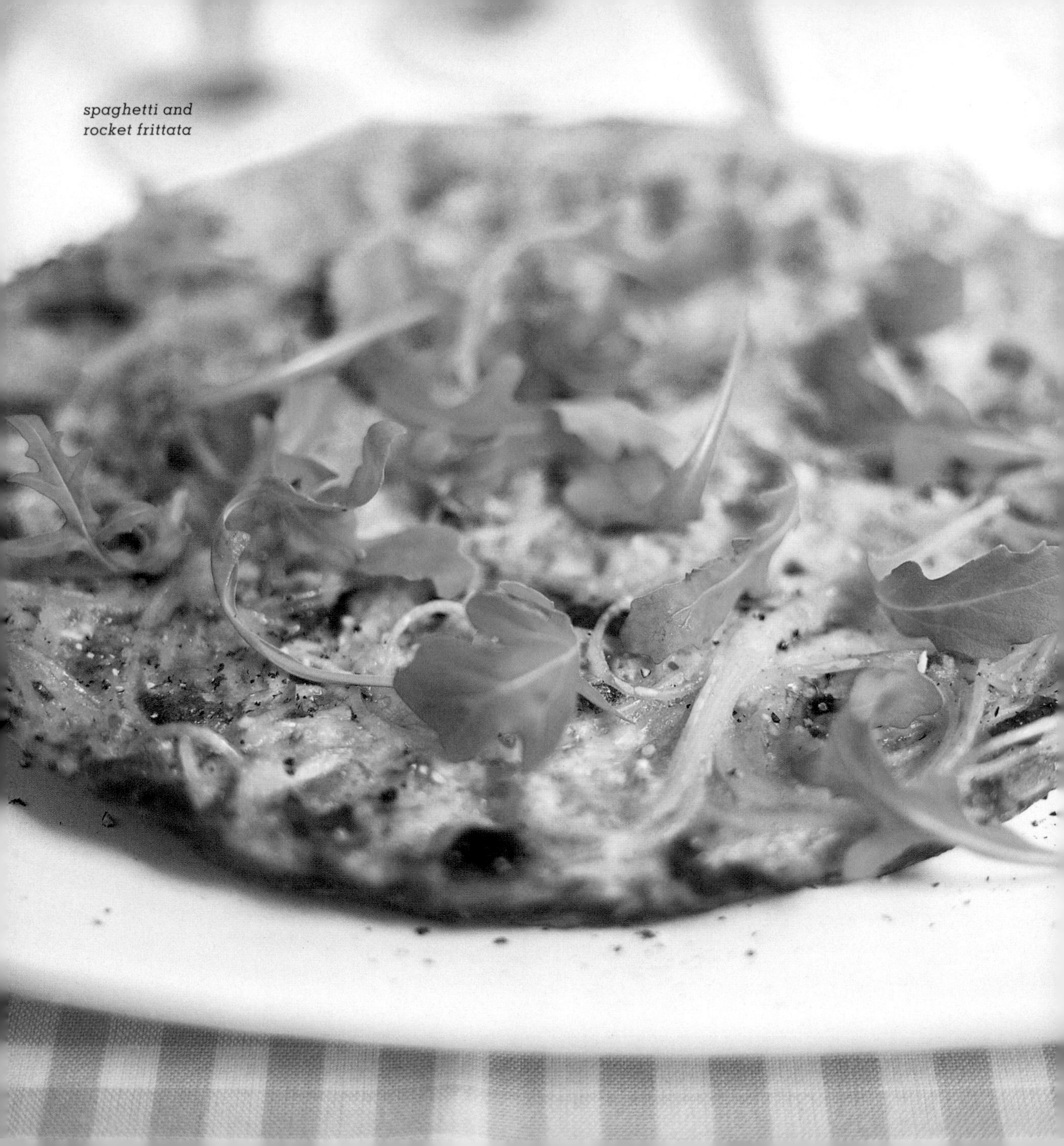
spaghetti and rocket frittata

spaghetti and rocket frittata

As with the frittata on page 145, this needs to be finished off under the grill so make sure your frying pan is ovenproof, and that the handle is away from the grill's direct heat.

As with the frittata on page 145,

serves
4

V

Heat 1 tablespoon of the oil in a saucepan, add the onion and sauté for 5 minutes until softened. Add the garlic, tomatoes and chilli and cook for 3–4 minutes. Add the tomato purée and wine or water and simmer for 5 minutes. Remove from the heat, add the spaghetti and toss gently.

Break the eggs into a large bowl and whisk briefly with a fork. Add the spaghetti and sauce and mix gently.

Heat the remaining oil in the frying pan, add the spaghetti and egg mixture and cook over low heat for 10–12 minutes, or until golden brown on the underside and almost set on the top. Meanwhile, preheat the grill.

Sprinkle the frittata with the Parmesan and slide under the grill for 30–60 seconds to melt the cheese and finish cooking the top. Leave to cool for 5 minutes, then transfer to a plate. Put the rocket leaves on top, drizzle with balsamic vinegar and serve immediately.

3 tablespoons olive oil

1 onion, chopped

1 garlic clove, crushed

3 ripe tomatoes, chopped

1 fresh red chilli, deseeded and finely chopped

2 tablespoons tomato purée

150 ml white wine or water

325 g cold cooked spaghetti (140 g before cooking)

6 large eggs

2 tablespoons grated Parmesan

25 g rocket

2 tablespoons balsamic vinegar

salt and black pepper

a 24-cm non-stick frying pan (measure the base, not the top)

parma ham-wrapped salmon with mash

This looks and tastes like food to impress, but it's effortless and has a very short shopping list.

serves
4

Q

F

Preheat the oven to 180°C (350°F) Gas 4.

Bring the potatoes to the boil in a pan of water, then simmer for 20 minutes, until soft. Drain and return to the pan, place over the heat and shake to remove any excess moisture. Mash well, then mix in the egg and seasoning. Add the butter and mash again until creamy.

Meanwhile, season the salmon fillets and wrap in the Parma ham. Place on the prepared baking tray and cook in the preheated oven for 15 minutes. Sprinkle with the dill and serve with the mashed potatoes.

800 g potatoes, unpeeled and diced

1 egg

50 g butter

4 salmon fillets, about 125 g each, skinned and boned

4 slices Parma ham

a bunch of fresh dill, chopped

salt and black pepper

a baking tray, lightly greased

fish baked with *lemon,* *oregano* and *potatoes*

serves
4

F

125 ml olive oil

2 onions, thinly sliced

2 garlic cloves, crushed

1–2 pinches of dried
chilli flakes

1 teaspoon crushed
coriander seeds

½ teaspoon dried oregano,
plus extra to serve

750 g potatoes,
cut into wedges

2 dried bay leaves

5 tablespoons white wine

½ teaspoon grated lemon zest

700–750 g any firm white fish,
skinned, boned and cut into
large chunks

2 small lemons, halved

1 tablespoon chopped
fresh flat leaf parsley

salt and black pepper

a large ovenproof dish

If you have a stovetop-to-oven pan, this dish can be cooked in one pot. Use chunks of firm white fish such as cod, haddock, hake or monkfish and choose potatoes that don't break up on cooking – large, waxy salad potatoes are ideal. As a rule of thumb, yellow-fleshed potatoes are waxy, while white potatoes tend to be floury. Some steamed greens tossed in a little olive oil make a great accompaniment to this dish.

Heat a large frying pan or ovenproof lidded skillet over medium heat and add the oil. Add the onion and fry for 2–3 minutes, then turn the heat down low. Add 1–2 pinches of salt, cover and let the onion cook very gently for 10–12 minutes until soft and golden yellow. Add the garlic, chilli flakes, crushed coriander seeds and oregano. Cook for another 3–4 minutes.

Add the potatoes and bay leaves to the pan, turning them in the oily onions. Season with 1 teaspoon salt and several turns of the pepper mill, cook for a few minutes, then add the wine and lemon zest. When it bubbles, cover and cook gently for 15–20 minutes or until the potatoes are just tender. Meanwhile, preheat the oven to 200°C (400°F) Gas 6.

Transfer the potatoes to the ovenproof dish, if necessary. Season the fish with a little salt, then nestle the fish into the potatoes. Squeeze a little lemon juice from one of the lemon halves over the fish and spoon over a little of the oily juices. Add the lemon halves to the dish and turn in the oil.

Bake, uncovered, in the preheated oven for 20–25 minutes, basting once or twice, until the potatoes are fully tender and the fish cooked through. The lemons should be touched with brown. Serve immediately, sprinkled with more oregano and the parsley.

flaked haddock moussaka

flaked *haddock* moussaka

This is one of those meals that is extremely comforting in the winter served with mashed potato, and yet works equally well in the summer alongside a large green salad.

serves
4

F

360 g haddock fillets, skinned and diced

1 teaspoon lemon juice

4 courgettes, thinly sliced

2 eggs

300 ml single cream

a pinch of freshly grated nutmeg

a little fresh dill, finely chopped

50 g Cheddar, grated

a shallow ovenproof dish, greased

a small roasting tin

Preheat the oven to 190°C (375°F) Gas 5.

Check the haddock for any remaining bones and discard them. Put the fish in the prepared ovenproof dish and sprinkle with the lemon juice.

Cook the courgettes for just 1 minute in boiling water, then drain, pat dry and place on top of the fish.

Beat the egg and cream together, add the nutmeg and dill and pour over the fish and courgettes. Put the dish in a small roasting tin half filled with cold water. Bake in the preheated oven for 45 minutes, or until the top is golden brown.

stir-fried *seafood* with *peppers* and *leeks*

Keeping a bag of mixed seafood in the freezer is a great standby for a fast supper. It can be added frozen to rice dishes, pasta or soup – just make sure it is cooked for a few minutes longer than fresh seafood, until piping hot.

serves
2

Q

F

2 tablespoons olive oil

1 red pepper, deseeded and cut into thin strips

2 leeks, cut into strips

1 large onion, cut into thick wedges

150 g cherry tomatoes, halved

2 garlic cloves, crushed

1 teaspoon dried chilli flakes

300 g frozen mixed seafood, such as prawns, mussels, scallops and squid rings, either defrosted or frozen

chopped fresh coriander, to serve

2 teaspoons balsamic vinegar

Heat 1 tablespoon of the oil in a large frying pan. Add the peppers, leeks and onion and stir-fry over high heat until lightly brown. Add the cherry tomatoes and cook for a further 2 minutes. Remove the vegetables from the pan and set aside in a warm place until needed.

Heat the remaining oil in the same frying pan. Add the garlic, chilli flakes and mixed seafood and stir-fry over high heat. Cook for 3–4 minutes, stirring occasionally (or cook for 7–8 minutes if the seafood is frozen).

Mix the warm vegetables with the seafood and add the balsamic vinegar and coriander at the last moment. Serve immediately.

600 g pork fillet, cut into
2-cm chunks

1 tablespoon light soy sauce

2 teaspoons finely grated
fresh ginger

2 tablespoons vegetable oil

1 large red pepper, deseeded
and cut into 2-cm chunks

1 large onion, cut into
8 wedges

½ large cucumber, roughly
peeled, halved, deseeded
and thickly sliced

300 g tinned pineapple, cut
into 2-cm chunks

Sauce

100 ml pineapple juice

4 tablespoons tomato ketchup

2 tablespoons rice vinegar

1 tablespoon light soy sauce

1 tablespoon caster sugar

1 tablespoon cornflour

sweet and sour *pork* with *pineapple* and *cucumber*

serves
4

M

A world away from the local takeaway's greasy battered nuggets drowned in a fluorescent gloop, this scrumptious recipe uses lean pork fillet, fried with cucumber wedges and juicy pineapple chunks and lightly coated in a sweet and tangy sauce. Serve it with your favourite accompaniment – rice, noodles or a pita or other flat bread to mop up the juices.

Combine all the sauce ingredients in a bowl and set aside.

Put the pork, soy sauce and ginger in a bowl and mix well. Cover and marinate in the fridge for 20 minutes, if possible.

Heat the oil in a large frying pan until hot, then add the pork in batches (don't over-crowd the pan, otherwise the pork will stew rather than fry). Stir-fry over high heat for 4–5 minutes until nearly cooked through and well sealed all over. Remove the pork from the pan and set aside.

Throw the red pepper and onion into the pan and stir-fry for 2–3 minutes. Return the pork to the pan with any juices. Pour in the sauce and toss everything together. Bring to the boil, then reduce the heat. Add the cucumber and pineapple and simmer gently for 3–4 minutes, or until the sauce has thickened and the pork is cooked through. Serve with the accompaniment of your choice.

quiche lorraine

Ready-made shortcrust pastry is available in supermarkets nowadays. It comes ready rolled or in a block. You'll need to weigh down the pastry when you bake it blind and for this you can use special ceramic baking beans, rice, dried beans or pasta.

serves
4–6

M

400 g shop-bought shortcrust pastry

200 g chopped bacon or cubed pancetta

5 eggs, plus 1 extra, lightly beaten with a fork, to glaze

200 ml double cream or crème fraîche

freshly grated nutmeg, to taste

50 g Gruyère, grated

salt and black pepper

a tart tin, 23 cm in diameter

baking beans, rice, dried beans or pasta, for blind baking

a baking tray

Preheat the oven to 200°C (400°F) Gas 6.

Roll out the pastry thinly on a lightly floured work surface until it is slightly bigger than the tart tin. Lay the pastry carefully over the tin and press it into shape all around the edges. Cut away any excess pastry with a knife. Prick the base all over with a fork, then chill or freeze for 15 minutes to set the pastry.

Line the base with aluminium foil and fill with baking beans or whatever you have chosen. Set on the baking tray and bake blind in the centre of the preheated oven for about 10–12 minutes. Remove the foil and baking beans and return the pastry case to the oven for a further 5–7 minutes to dry out completely. To prevent the pastry from becoming soggy, brush the blind-baked case with the beaten egg – you can do this when it is hot or cold. Bake again for 5–10 minutes until set and shiny. This will also fill and seal any holes made when pricking before the blind baking.

Heat a non-stick frying pan and fry the bacon or pancetta until brown and crisp, then drain on kitchen paper. Scatter over the base of the pastry case.

Put the eggs and cream into a bowl, beat well, and season with salt, pepper and nutmeg to taste. Carefully pour the mixture over the bacon and sprinkle with the Gruyère.

Bake for about 25 minutes until just set, golden brown and puffy. Serve warm or at room temperature.

sausage, sun-dried tomato and *potato* tart

serves
4–6

M

450 g shop-bought shortcrust pastry

1 egg, lightly beaten with a fork, to glaze

Sausage and onion filling

350 g sausages

3 tablespoons olive oil

3 onions, thinly sliced

2 garlic cloves, crushed

200 g potatoes, chopped

1 tablespoon plain flour

2–3 tablespoons tomato purée

12 sun-dried tomato halves in oil, chopped

1 teaspoon dried chilli flakes

2 teaspoons dried Herbes de Provence

150 g mascarpone

salt and black pepper

a tart tin, 24 cm in diameter and 4 cm deep

baking beans, rice, dried beans or pasta, for blind baking

a baking tray

There is a fabulous blend of flavours in this tart. The mascarpone is dotted onto the sausage mixture before the onions are piled on top – so it just melts in.

Bring the pastry to room temperature. Meanwhile, preheat the oven to 200°C (400°F) Gas 6.

Roll out the pastry thinly on a lightly floured work surface until it is slightly bigger than the tart tin. Lay the pastry carefully over the tin and press it into shape all around the edges. Cut away any excess pastry with a knife. Prick the base all over with a fork, then chill or freeze for 15 minutes to set the pastry.

Line the base with aluminium foil and fill with baking beans or whatever you have chosen. Set on the baking tray and bake blind in the centre of the preheated oven for about 10–12 minutes. Remove the foil and baking beans and return the pastry case to the oven for a further 5–7 minutes to dry out completely. To prevent the pastry from becoming soggy, brush the blind-baked case with the beaten egg – you can do this when it is hot or cold. Bake again for 5–10 minutes until set and shiny. This will also fill and seal any holes made when pricking before the blind baking.

To make the sausage and onion filling, cut away the skins of the sausages and pull the sausagemeat into chunks. Heat the oil in a large saucepan, add the onions, garlic and 3 tablespoons water. Cover and cook over gentle heat for about 1 hour or until meltingly soft but not coloured. Stir the onions occasionally and watch for catching. Leave the onions to cool.

Blanch the potatoes in boiling salted water for 1 minute, then drain and set aside. Heat a non-stick frying pan and add the sausagemeat, breaking it up with a wooden spoon as it cooks and browns. After about 5 minutes, stir in the flour, tomato purée, sun-dried tomatoes, chilli flakes, herbs, and salt and pepper to taste. Cook for another 5 minutes, then stir in the potatoes. Spoon this into the pastry case and dot small spoonfuls of the mascarpone over the surface. Cover with a layer of the cooked onions, then bake for 25 minutes until the onions are golden.

*cumin-spiced
lamb cutlets*

roast *potatoes*, *chorizo* and *lemon*

Simple roast potatoes are endlessly popular, but sometimes it's fun to jazz them up with extra flavour.

Preheat the oven to 200°C (400°F) Gas 6.

Cut the potatoes into large pieces. Put in a large saucepan and cover with water. Bring to the boil and boil for 5 minutes. Drain in a colander or sieve and leave to dry out for 5 minutes. Toss the potatoes around in the sieve or colander to rough up the outsides.

Pour the oil into the roasting tin. Heat in the preheated oven for 5 minutes. Add the potatoes and garlic to the hot oil with plenty of salt and stir well to coat. Roast for 20 minutes, then remove the tin from the oven, stir again and add the chorizo, lemon and rosemary. Return to the hot oven and continue roasting for a further 20 minutes. Serve immediately.

serves
6

Q

M

1 kg potatoes

3 whole garlic bulbs,
cut in half crossways

3 tablespoons olive oil

3 small chorizo sausages,
diagonally sliced

1 lemon, halved lengthways
and sliced

2 tablespoons fresh
rosemary needles

salt

a large roasting tin

cumin-spiced *lamb* cutlets

Here are some lemony, minty grilled lamb cutlets accompanied by ultra-easy chickpea mash made with tinned chickpeas.

To make the marinade, combine the olive oil, mint, lemon zest and 1 tablespoon of the juice, the chilli powder and garlic in a large bowl. Add the lamb cutlets, season well with salt and pepper and toss. If you have time, marinate for an hour; if not, move swiftly on.

Heat ½ tablespoon of the olive oil in a frying pan, add the cumin seeds and stir for 30 seconds until fragrant. Tip in the chickpeas and toss in the oil for 1 minute. Stir in the remaining lemon juice and 100 ml water, cover and simmer for 10 minutes until softened. Meanwhile, preheat the grill to high.

Put the lamb cutlets on the prepared baking tray and grill for 5–6 minutes until charred around the edges. Turn over, add the tomatoes, drizzle with the remaining olive oil, season and grill for 5–6 minutes.

Mash the chickpeas with a potato masher until you get a chunky purée. Add the coriander, season to taste and stir. Transfer to bowls and top with 3 lamb cutlets. Drizzle with the lamb juices.

serves
4

M

12 medium lamb cutlets

2 tablespoons olive oil

1 teaspoon cumin seeds

2 x 400-g tins chickpeas,
drained

300 g cherry tomatoes

4 tablespoons chopped
fresh coriander

salt and black pepper

Marinade

2 tablespoons olive oil

2 tablespoons chopped
fresh mint

finely grated zest of 1 unwaxed
lemon, plus 5 tablespoons juice

1 teaspoon chilli powder

1 garlic clove, crushed

*a baking tray, lined with
aluminium foil*

mince and
pea curry

beef
rendang

2 tablespoons sunflower oil

1 large onion, finely chopped

3 garlic cloves, crushed

1 teaspoon finely grated
fresh ginger

3–4 green chillies (deseeded
if desired), thinly sliced

1 tablespoon cumin seeds

3 tablespoons medium
curry paste

800 g minced beef

400-g tin chopped tomatoes

1 teaspoon sugar

4 tablespoons tomato purée

4 tablespoons coconut cream

250 g frozen peas

salt and black pepper

a large handful of fresh
coriander leaves, chopped,
to garnish

mince and *pea* curry

serves
4

M

Minced meat is cooked slowly with spices and peas resulting in
a subtle, fragrant curry, which is great when accompanied by
either Spiced Aubergine Dahl (page 145), steamed basmati rice
or naan bread – or all of the above!

Heat the sunflower oil in a large, heavy-based saucepan and add the onion.
Cook over low heat for 15–20 minutes, until softened and just turning light
golden. Add the garlic, ginger, chillies, cumin seeds and curry paste and
stir-fry over high heat for 1–2 minutes.

Add the minced beef and stir-fry for 3–4 minutes, then stir in the tinned
tomatoes, sugar, and tomato purée and bring to the boil. Season well, cover
and reduce the heat to low. Cook for 1–1½ hours. 10 minutes before the end
of the cooking time, add the coconut cream and peas.

To serve, garnish with the coriander and serve with accompaniments of
your choice.

beef rendang

This is a gentle, aromatic meat curry from Indonesia made all in one pot, with diced beef. Tamarind purée is sold in small jars from supermarkets or Asian stores. Like all the best curries, this one needs to cook slowly and gently on the hob so that the meat has time to tenderize and absorb the flavours from the spices. Serve it with Thai jasmine rice and green beans.

serves
4

M

500 g diced braising steak

1 tablespoon tamarind purée

1 cinnamon stick

1 tablespoon dark muscovado sugar

2 tablespoons soy sauce

250 ml hot beef or vegetable stock

¼ teaspoon ground black pepper

¼ teaspoon freshly grated nutmeg

6 green cardamom pods

2 red onions, very finely chopped

3 garlic cloves, crushed

3-cm piece of fresh ginger, peeled and finely chopped

Put the meat in a heavy medium saucepan or casserole dish. Add the tamarind, cinnamon stick, sugar, soy sauce, stock, pepper and nutmeg.

Crush the cardamom pods with a mortar and pestle (or with the end of a rolling pin). Throw away the green husks and keep the tiny black seeds. Crush the seeds and add to the pan with the onions, garlic and ginger. Stir until well mixed.

Set the pan over medium heat and bring the mixture to the boil. Stir, then cover the pan with a lid and turn down the heat to very low so the mixture bubbles very gently.

Leave to cook for 1½ hours, stirring now and then.

Finally, remove the lid and cook uncovered for 20–30 minutes until the sauce is very thick. Remove the cinnamon stick and serve.

steak with new potatoes, roquefort and rocket

700 g new potatoes

4 x 250-g sirloin or rib-eye steaks (2 cm thick)

5 tablespoons olive oil

1 garlic clove, crushed

2 tablespoons capers

finely grated zest and juice of 1 unwaxed lemon

50 g rocket

75 g Roquefort

salt and black pepper

a ridged griddle pan (optional)

serves
4

M

Cooking steaks well is all about getting the pan very hot and creating a golden crust on the meat which prevents any juices from escaping. Leave them to rest after cooking and squeeze over lemon juice (an Italian trick), which cuts through the richness of the meat. When finishing the potatoes, don't be stingy with the olive oil: use a liberal amount of good-quality oil as it's not being cooked so you really taste the flavours.

Put a medium saucepan of water on to boil. Add a large pinch of salt and the potatoes. Simmer gently for 20–22 minutes until very tender, then drain and return to the pan.

Meanwhile, heat the griddle pan or a large frying pan over very high heat. Drizzle the steaks with 1 tablespoon of the olive oil and season. When the pan is smoking, add the steaks. Leave them to cook, without turning them over, for 3 minutes. Now turn them over and cook for a further 2–3 minutes. Prod them to check if they are done to your liking: a little give means medium and lots of give means rare. Transfer them to a plate, cover with aluminium foil and leave to rest for a few minutes.

Mix the remaining olive oil with the garlic, capers and lemon zest in a small jug, season well and set aside. Lightly crush the potatoes with the back of a spoon until they buckle a little, then fold in the rocket and olive oil. Crumble over the Roquefort cheese and transfer to bowls. Pour the lemon juice all over the steaks and cut into strips. Lift onto the potatoes, pour over any steak juices and grind over some pepper.

beef fajitas with *guacamole* and *soured cream*

Since your friends can help themselves and put together their own traditional fajitas, this dish is terrifically straightforward to serve. If you like a very spicy guacamole, add a couple of extra jalapeño chillies, deseeded and finely chopped.

Preheat the oven to 170°C (325°F) Gas 3.

Remove any fat from the beef and cut it diagonally, across the grain, to create finger length strips. Mix together 2 tablespoons of oil, the pimentón and cumin in a large bowl. Add the beef pieces and toss until evenly coated in the spiced oil. Set aside.

Heat a large frying pan over high heat with the remaining oil and stir-fry the red onion, red or green pepper and garlic for 3–4 minutes, until they start to go limp and the edges begin to char. Remove from the pan and set aside in a warm place.

Wrap the tortillas in aluminium foil and place them in the preheated oven to warm for about 5 minutes. (Alternatively, you can follow the manufacturer's instructions for warming them in a microwave.)

Meanwhile, wipe the frying pan clean with kitchen paper. Heat until smoking hot, then drop the strips of meat into the pan over high heat, working in batches and turning them frequently. Each batch should take no more than 1–2 minutes to cook. Season the meat with salt and pepper.

To serve, arrange the beef strips, guacamole, peppers, onion, jalapeño chillies, rocket, soured cream and hot chilli sauce, if using, in separate bowls. Wrap the tortillas in a cloth napkin and put them in a basket or dish (so that they don't dry out and go hard) and bring them to the table. Let everyone dig in.

serves
4–6

M

4 x 200-g sirloin steaks (2.5 cm thick)

4 tablespoons olive oil

1 tablespoon pimentón (Spanish oak-smoked paprika)

1 tablespoon ground cumin

1 large red onion, cut into petals

1 red or green pepper, deseeded and thinly sliced

3 garlic cloves, thinly sliced

8–12 soft wheat or cornflour tortillas

salt and black pepper

To serve

Guacamole (page 19)

100 g jalapeño chillies, deseeded and chopped

a handful of rocket

hot chilli sauce (optional)

soured cream

lemony poached *chicken*

2 small, unwaxed lemons, each cut into 6 wedges

a 2.5-kg chicken

30 ml olive oil

1 whole garlic bulb, cloves separated but left unpeeled

a small bunch of fresh sage

1 litre milk

salt and black pepper

bread, to serve

serves
6

M

This recipe is for a whole chicken. After an hour on the hob, the chicken is fabulously juicy and the sauce is sticky and lemony.

Season the chicken all over with salt and pepper. Heat half the olive oil in a large saucepan and cook the chicken, breast-side down, for 4–5 minutes, until golden. Turn the chicken over and cook for 3–4 minutes more. Remove the chicken from the pan and pour away any used oil. Pour the remaining olive oil into the pan and add the lemon wedges and garlic. Stir-fry for 2–3 minutes, until golden. Add the sage and cook for another minute or so.

Return the chicken to the pan and pour the milk over it. Put a lid on the pan, leaving a little opening to allow the steam to escape. Simmer over gentle heat for about 1 hour, until the meat is cooked through and the sauce has curdled into sticky nuggets (keep the heat low, or the milk will reduce too quickly to cook the chicken). Remove the pan from the heat. Leave to rest for 4–5 minutes before slicing. Serve warm with chunks of bread to mop up the sauce. Squeeze the softened garlic out and spread onto the bread.

beefburgers

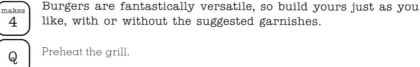

600 g minced beef

1 garlic clove, crushed

1 shallot, finely diced

a bunch of fresh parsley, chopped

1 tablespoon olive oil

1 teaspoon Worcestershire sauce

4 rashers of streaky bacon

4 ciabatta rolls

4 tablespoons mayonnaise

4 slices of beef tomato

100 g Cheddar, grated

1 avocado, sliced

shredded iceberg lettuce

salt and black pepper

makes
4

Q

M

Burgers are fantastically versatile, so build yours just as you like, with or without the suggested garnishes.

Preheat the grill.

Put the beef, garlic, shallot, parsley and Worcestershire sauce in a large bowl, season with salt and pepper and mix well with your hands. Divide the mixture into 4 and shape into burgers.

Heat some oil in a large frying pan and cook for 2 minutes on each side for rare, 3 minutes for medium-rare and 4 minutes for well done.

Meanwhile, grill the bacon until crisp. Cut the ciabatta rolls in half and grill the insides. Spread the grilled sides with mayonnaise. Put a slice of tomato on the grilled base and a burger on top, followed by a handful of cheese, a bacon rasher, a slice or two of avocado and some lettuce. Sandwich together with the remaining bread and serve with ketchup and mustard.

italian *roast chicken*

This is a dead easy Sunday roast and there's no excuse not to give it a try: the smell of roasting chicken is, after all, irresistible, plus, because this dish uses chicken pieces, there's no difficult carving, and the gravy magically appears during cooking. Choose chicken legs if you're hungry, otherwise large thighs, because these have the most flavour. Serve with Roasties (page 195) or pasta and a green vegetable or a leafy salad.

4 chicken legs or thighs

4 garlic cloves, unpeeled

juice of 1 large lemon

2 tablespoons olive oil

4 large sprigs of fresh thyme or rosemary

salt and black pepper

1 or 2 ovenproof dishes, big enough to hold the chicken in one layer

Preheat the oven to 220°C (425°F) Gas 6.

Put the chicken pieces into the ovenproof dishes, skin side up, and check that the pieces don't overlap each other. Put the garlic cloves in the dishes between the chicken pieces. Pour the lemon juice all over the chicken, then pour the oil over the top so the skin is evenly coated in liquid. Sprinkle with 4 pinches of salt and then about 3 turns of the pepper grinder. Finally, set a sprig of thyme or rosemary on the top of each piece of chicken.

Put the chicken in the preheated oven. Roast for 40 minutes for large legs, and 35 minutes for thighs. As the chicken cooks, the legs become a crispy golden brown, surrounded by a light brown cooking-juice gravy. Make sure the juices run clear and the meat is fully cooked before removing from the oven. Serve with Roasties and gravy from the dishes.

2 tablespoons olive oil

2 kg chicken pieces, such as legs, thighs and wings

8 garlic cloves, thinly sliced

400-g tin chopped tomatoes

a pinch of sugar

50 g stoned black olives, roughly chopped

salt and black pepper

a bunch of fresh basil, torn

chicken with tomato, garlic and olives

serves 4–6

M

Here's another effortless option for cooking a large quantity of chicken to feed hungry, appreciative friends, but it's cooked on the hob rather than roasted. It goes well with rice or pasta.

Heat 1 tablespoon of the oil in a large saucepan. Add the chicken pieces and brown on all sides. Transfer the chicken to a plate, salt generously and set aside. Add the remaining oil and garlic and cook for 1 minute, then add the tomatoes and sugar. Stir well and return the chicken to the pan. Cover and simmer gently until the chicken is cooked, 25–30 minutes. Transfer to a serving dish, then raise the heat and cook the sauce to thicken slightly, about 10 minutes. Add salt and pepper to taste, then stir in the olives. Pour the sauce over the chicken and sprinkle with the basil.

800 g boneless, skinless chicken thighs, cut into bite-sized pieces

500 g frozen spinach, thawed

2 tablespoons sunflower oil

1 onion, finely chopped

2 teaspoons cumin seeds

150 ml hot chicken stock

1 tablespoon lemon juice

salt and black pepper

Marinade

100 g natural yoghurt (not low-fat)

2 tablespoons crushed garlic

2 tablespoons finely grated fresh ginger

2 tablespoons ground coriander

2 tablespoons medium curry powder

chicken and spinach curry

serves 4

M

This is a velvety curry which needs some forward planning as the chicken has to marinate for 3–4 hours or overnight.

To make the marinade, combine the yoghurt, garlic, ginger, coriander and curry powder in a large glass bowl and season well. Stir in the chicken, cover and refrigerate for 3–4 hours or overnight.

Put the spinach in a saucepan and cook for 8–10 minutes. Drain thoroughly, then chop as finely as possible. Season well with salt and pepper.

Heat the oil in a large, non-stick frying pan and add the onion. Cook over gentle heat for 10–12 minutes. Add the cumin seeds and stir-fry for 1–2 minutes. Increase the heat to high and add the marinated chicken (discarding the marinade). Stir-fry for 6–8 minutes. Pour in the stock and spinach and bring to the boil. Reduce the heat to low, cover tightly and cook for 25–30 minutes, or until the chicken is cooked through.

Uncover the pan, check the seasoning and cook over high heat for 3–4 minutes, stirring often. Remove from the heat and stir in the lemon.

chicken with tomato,
garlic and olives

roast chicken with garlic, apple and cider

This is the roast to choose when there are just two of you and it's a bit of a special occasion. Don't be alarmed by the amount of garlic that goes into the dish – the flavour becomes much more subtle once the garlic is blanched. Serve with broccoli and new potatoes.

Preheat the oven to 200°C (400°F) Gas 6.

Bring a small pan of water to the boil and cook the garlic cloves for 2–3 minutes, or until tender. Drain and set aside until needed.

Season the chicken breasts and drizzle with the olive oil. Put them on the baking tray and place on the top shelf of the preheated oven to cook for about 25 minutes, or until the chicken is cooked through and the skin is golden.

Meanwhile, put the garlic, cider, chopped apple and mustard in a large frying pan. Cook gently over low heat for about 10 minutes.

When the chicken is cooked, remove it from the oven and transfer to the pan. Add the crème fraîche to the pan and simmer for 5 minutes. Use the back of a fork to squash the garlic down into the sauce, taking care not to squash the apples too. Season with salt and pepper to taste. Stir in the parsley and serve immediately, with broccoli and new potatoes.

Variation This classic French sauce also tastes really good served with oven-roasted or grilled pork chops.

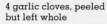

serves
2

M

4 garlic cloves, peeled but left whole

2 skinless chicken breast fillets (each about 130 g)

2 tablespoons olive oil

100 ml dry cider

1 red apple, peeled, cored and diced

2 tablespoons Dijon mustard

100 ml crème fraîche

a handful of chopped fresh parsley

salt and black pepper

purple sprouting broccoli spears and new potatoes, to serve

a baking tray

4 skinless and boneless chicken thighs, diced

2 large leeks, cut into chunks

2 garlic cloves, crushed

150 ml hot chicken stock

grated zest and juice of ½ unwaxed lemon

1 teaspoon dried tarragon

400-g tin haricot beans, drained and rinsed

200 g fine green beans

2 tablespoons crème fraîche

salt and black pepper

tarragon chicken casserole

serves
4

M

A good casserole is hard to beat, especially on a cold winter's evening. It tends to taste even better the following day so treat yourself to the leftovers with some crusty bread.

Season the chicken with salt and pepper and dry-fry in a non-stick frying pan for 3 minutes until browned. Transfer to a casserole dish or large saucepan. Add the leeks and garlic to the frying pan with 2 tablespoons of the stock and cook for 2 minutes, then tip into the casserole dish.

Pour the remaining stock into the casserole dish and add the lemon zest and juice, tarragon and haricot beans. Bring to a simmer, cover and cook gently for 15 minutes.

Stir in the green beans, re-cover and cook for a further 15 minutes until the beans are tender but still have some bite. Finally, stir in the crème fraîche just before serving.

1 garlic clove, peeled but left whole

melted butter, for brushing

400 g parsnips, cut into 1-cm diagonal slices

a handful of fresh sage leaves

350 g carrots, cut into 1-cm diagonal slices

350 g uncooked beetroot, scrubbed well and cut into 1-cm diagonal slices

275 ml double cream

1 tablespoon olive oil

salt and black pepper

an ovenproof dish

roasted *vegetable* dauphinois

serves
4

V

This rich, creamy, garlicky sauce is offset by the earthy flavours of root vegetables. It is incredibly straightforward to make and it's delicious served with lamb or beef.

Preheat the oven to 200°C (400°F) Gas 6.

Rub the garlic around the base and sides of the ovenproof dish, then brush with melted butter. Pack overlapping slices of parsnips into the dish. Season well with salt and pepper, then add one-third of the sage leaves. Repeat the process, first with the carrots, then the beetroot, seasoning each layer with salt and pepper and dotting with the remaining sage. Pour in the cream.

Cover the dish with aluminium foil and bake in the preheated oven for 1 hour 40 minutes. Remove the foil and lightly sprinkle the top with the olive oil. Return to the oven and continue cooking for a further 20 minutes or until the vegetables are very tender.

*roasted vegetable
dauphinois*

roasties

roasties

It's hard to imagine a roast dinner without crunchy roast potatoes, not to mention roast parsnips, roast sweet potatoes and more. So here is an easy way to cook all your favourite vegetables in one roasting tin.

serves 4–6

V

500 g baking potatoes, cut into chunks

500 g parsnips, cut into chunks

500 g sweet potatoes, cut into chunks

500 g large carrots, cut into chunks

3 tablespoons olive oil

salt and black pepper

3 sprigs of fresh thyme or rosemary (or both)

a large roasting tin

Preheat the oven to 220°C (425°F) Gas 7.

Put all the vegetables in the roasting tin. Pour the oil over the top, sprinkle with the salt and pepper, then add the herbs, pushing them between the vegetables. Using both hands, toss the vegetables in the oil and seasonings so they are very well mixed. Spread out the vegetables so they are in a single layer.

Bake in the preheated oven for about 1 hour, but every 15 minutes during the cooking time, remove the tin carefully from the oven and gently turn over the vegetables so they cook and brown evenly.

At the end of the cooking time, transfer the roasties to a serving dish, removing any large sprigs of thyme or rosemary.

potatoes boulangère

Finely sliced potatoes cooked in a stock and allowed to dry and crisp on top: edible heaven.

serves 4

V

1 kg floury potatoes, sliced

2 onions, finely sliced

300 ml hot vegetable stock

25 g butter, finely diced

salt and black pepper

a 23-cm shallow, ovenproof dish, greased

Preheat the oven to 180°C (350°F) Gas 4.

Put a layer of potatoes in the buttered dish, then add a layer of onions. Season well with salt and pepper, then repeat the layers until all the ingredients are used. Finish with a neat layer of potatoes overlapping each other and push down firmly.

Pour on the hot stock and dot the top with the butter. Bake in the preheated oven for about 1½ hours or until the top is golden brown and crunchy and the potatoes are soft right through when tested with the point of a knife.

sweet things

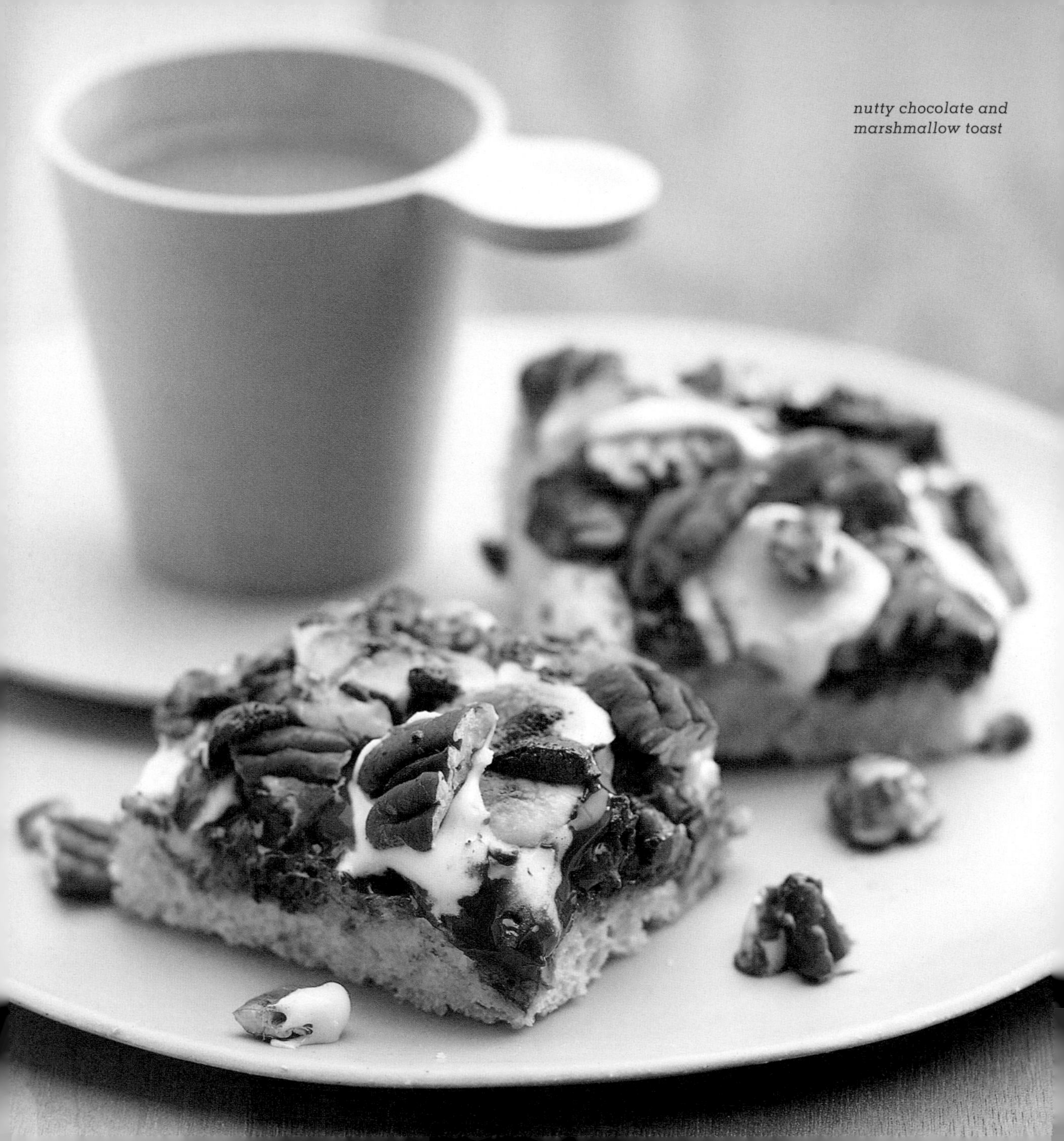

nutty chocolate and marshmallow toast

nutty *chocolate* and *marshmallow* toast

Sinfully sweet and sticky, this toast is the ultimate in instant comfort food. It's lacking sophistication by anyone's standards – but it makes a luscious treat when you're feeling blue and need a no-effort pick-me-up.

Preheat the grill.

Toast the bread on one side under the grill, then flip over. Pour the cream over the untoasted side, sprinkle with the grated or shaved chocolate, nuts and marshmallows and grill until golden and bubbling. Eat with caution: the topping will be hot!

Note You can use any type of white bread – a classic square white loaf, a white bloomer or several slices of white baguette cut diagonally.

serves **2**

Q

V

2 thick slices of white bread

2 tablespoons single cream

15 g plain chocolate, grated or shaved, or plain chocolate chips

15 g shelled pecan nuts

25 g mini-marshmallows

toasted oat yoghurt and *crushed red berries*

Baking the oats adds a caramel crunch to this simple pudding. If you don't have red berries you can use whatever fruit you have to hand – bananas, apples, peaches or nectarines are all good.

Preheat the grill.

Put the rolled oats and sugar into a bowl and mix. Sprinkle evenly over the baking tray and put under the grill. Toast until golden and caramelized, then remove and leave to cool on the tray.

Put half the berries into a bowl and coarsely crush with the back of a spoon. Add the yoghurt and oats and mix lightly until marbled. Spoon into glasses and top with the remaining berries and honey. Chill until ready to serve.

serves **4**

Q

V

50 g rolled oats

20 g brown sugar

300 g fresh red berries

200 ml Greek yoghurt

4 tablespoons runny honey

a baking tray, lined with greaseproof paper

french *pancakes*

makes
12

V

It's great fun (and less work for you) to set up a 'pancake bar' on the kitchen table and let everyone help themselves to their favourite topping (see below).

100 g plain flour

1 large egg

300 ml milk

a little butter or vegetable oil, for frying

Put the flour in a large bowl and make a hollow in the middle. Crack the egg into the hollow and start to whisk it in with a balloon whisk. Gradually pour in the milk and continue to whisk until the batter is well mixed and smooth. Cover and chill for 30 minutes. (The batter can be made in advance and kept for up to 24 hours.)

Wipe a frying pan with the butter and heat. Add a ladleful of batter, tilting the pan to spread it evenly. Cook for 1–2 minutes on each side until light brown. Stack the pancakes on a large plate and keep warm.

pancake toppings

The simplest ideas are often the best, so here are some quick and easy toppings.

Quick chocolate sauce

150 g plain chocolate

2 tablespoons golden syrup

70 g unsalted butter

1 tablespoon brandy (optional)

Put all the ingredients in a small saucepan and melt over low heat, stirring continuously until smooth.

Lemon and sugar

The classic way of serving pancakes: squeeze some lemon juice over the top and sprinkle with a little sugar.

Honey and walnuts

Offer a pot of runny honey with a drizzler and a little dish of chopped walnuts for scattering.

Fruit jam and crème fraîche

Spread raspberry or strawberry jam on the pancake and top generously with crème fraîche.

muffin mania

Use this basic recipe to create different kinds of flavoured muffins. If you prepare the dry mix the day before, you can quickly rustle up some freshly-baked muffins in the morning.

makes
6

V

250 g plain flour

125 g caster sugar

1 tablespoon baking powder

½ teaspoon salt

1 large egg

125 ml milk (or a little more)

50 ml sunflower oil

a 6- or 12-hole muffin tin, lined with paper cases

Preheat the oven to 180°C (350°F) Gas 4.

Sift the flour, sugar, baking powder and salt together into a large bowl or plastic bag.

Whisk the egg in a large bowl with a balloon whisk, then whisk in the milk and oil. Add the dry ingredients and stir with a wooden spoon until just blended. The mixture should look very coarse with lumps and floury pockets. This will make the muffins light and fluffy when they're baked.

Spoon into the cases in the muffin tin, filling them three-quarters full. Bake in the preheated oven for about 20 minutes or until well risen and golden brown.

Remove from the oven and leave for a couple of minutes, then pop the muffins out of the tin. Serve warm – they do not reheat well.

Variations

• Experiment with different flours, and adjust the liquid accordingly because wholemeal flours tend to absorb more liquid.
• Add nuts, seeds and dried fruits to the basic mixture.
• Use soft brown sugar instead of caster sugar.
• Sift in spices with the dry ingredients.
• Quickly stir whole berries or chopped fresh fruit into the mix before baking.
• For a crunchy topping, mix chopped nuts and seeds into soft brown sugar and sprinkle on top of the muffins before baking.

double *chocolate* muffins

250 g plain flour

40 g cocoa powder

100 g caster sugar

2 teaspoons baking powder

80 g chocolate chips,
plus extra for sprinkling

2 large eggs

230 ml milk

125 ml sunflower oil

1 teaspoon vanilla extract

a 12-hole deep muffin tin,
lined with paper cases

makes
12

V

Everybody loves chocolate muffins! These are very quick to whip up and made with cocoa powder plus chocolate chips for maximum chocolate flavour. The brilliant thing about muffins is how versatile they are, and how popular. Bake a batch and take them round to a friend who is down-in-the-dumps, make a large number for hungry revellers at a house party, or keep a few in the freezer for days when you crave a chocolatey treat.

Preheat the oven to 200°C (400°F) Gas 6.

Sift the flour, cocoa powder, sugar and baking powder together into a large bowl or plastic bag. Add the chocolate chips.

Whisk the eggs in a large bowl with a balloon whisk, then whisk in the milk, oil and vanilla. Add the dry ingredients and stir with a wooden spoon until just blended. The mixture should look very coarse with lumps and floury pockets. This will make the muffins light and fluffy when they're baked.

Spoon into the cases in the muffin tin, filling them about half full. Dot the chocolate chips over the top. Bake in the preheated oven for about 20 minutes or until well risen and just firm. The chocolate chips become very hot, so take care not to touch them.

Remove from the oven and leave for a couple of minutes, then pop the muffins out of the tin. Serve warm – they do not reheat well.

cheat's cherry brûlée

cheat's *cherry* brûlée

Real crème brûlée is creamy, indulgent and a bit fiddly to make. This is the cheat's alternative. Don't be put off by needing fancy crème fraîche and fromage frais – they are now both easy to find in your local supermarket and you can use up any leftovers with freshly chopped fruit for breakfast.

serves **4**

Q

V

300 g fresh, ripe cherries, stoned

100 ml crème fraîche

100 ml fromage frais

1 teaspoon vanilla extract

4 tablespoons demerara sugar

4 ramekins, 150 ml each

Preheat the grill.

Put the cherries in a saucepan with 100 ml water. Cook over high heat until simmering, then lower the heat and simmer gently until the fruit is slightly softened, 5–7 minutes. Remove the pan from the heat.

Put the crème fraîche, fromage frais and vanilla in a bowl and mix well. Divide the cherries between the 4 ramekins. Spoon the cream mixture over the cherries, then top each serving with 1 tablespoon of the demerara sugar.

Put the ramekins under the grill until the sugar melts and begins to caramelize. Remove from the heat and serve immediately.

plum clafoutis

For a very decadent pudding, use single cream instead of milk in this recipe. You can also use other stone fruits or berries.

serves **4**

V

750 g plums, halved and stoned

4 eggs

500 ml milk

75 g plain flour

75 g caster sugar

icing sugar, to dust

a shallow ovenproof dish, 25 cm square, lightly greased

Preheat the oven to 190°C (375°F) Gas 5.

Arrange the halved plums in the prepared dish. Beat the eggs in a jug, add the milk and mix well.

Sift the flour into a medium bowl, add the sugar and make a well in the centre. Slowly whisk in the milk mixture until it is all incorporated and the batter is smooth and glossy.

Pour the batter over the plums and bake in the preheated oven for about 40 minutes until golden and firm to the touch.

Lightly dust the clafoutis with icing sugar just before serving.

grilled *peaches* with *pistachios* and *dates*

2 heaped tablespoons cream cheese

2 teaspoons orange juice

10 shelled pistachio nuts or other favourite nuts, roughly chopped

2 stoned dried dates, finely chopped

2 ripe peaches or nectarines

A deliciously moreish, easy pudding of peaches stuffed with a creamy, nutritious date and nut filling. The perfect treat for those who don't want to spend long in the kitchen.

Preheat the grill and line the grill pan with aluminium foil.

Meanwhile, mix together the cream cheese, orange juice, pistachios and dates in a small bowl. Cut the peaches in half, twist to separate the fruit into halves, then prise out the stones.

Spoon the cream cheese mixture into the peach centres. Grill for 6–7 minutes until the cream cheese mixture starts to turn golden and the fruit softens.

baked amaretti *peaches* with *raspberry* sauce

3 tablespoons unsalted butter, at room temperature

3 tablespoons caster sugar

1 large egg

40 g ground almonds

30 g finely crushed amaretti biscuits, about 4 small ones

6 ripe peaches

Greek yoghurt or crème fraîche, to serve

Raspberry sauce

250 g fresh raspberries (or frozen and defrosted)

1 tablespoon icing sugar

1 tablespoon lemon juice

a 12-hole muffin tin (optional)

These must be eaten soon after baking, but the filling can be made in advance and chilled until needed. If you don't have a muffin tin, make rings out of foil to keep the peaches upright.

Preheat the oven to 180°C (350°F) Gas 4.

Put the butter and sugar in a bowl and beat until blended. Beat in the egg. Stir in the ground almonds and amaretti until well mixed. Set aside.

Cut the peaches in half, twist to separate the fruit into halves, then prise out the stones. Scrape out a bit more from each hollow to make more space for the filling. Divide the filling between the peaches. Put a peach half into each muffin hole to keep them upright while baking.

Bake in the preheated oven until the filling is puffed and golden, about 25–30 minutes. To make the raspberry sauce, mash the raspberries, icing sugar and lemon juice together in a bowl. Serve the peaches warm, with yoghurt and the raspberry sauce.

grilled peaches with
pistachios and dates

chocolate brownies

Who doesn't love chocolate brownies? They're pretty easy to make but the skill is in the timing: it's easy to think your brownies aren't cooked and to give them those extra few minutes in the oven, which can dry them out and turn them into a mealy chocolate cake. So be brave – if the mixture doesn't wobble in the middle and a skewer inserted in the centre comes out chocolatey, remove the brownies from the oven and by the time they have cooled, they will be perfect.

makes
16

V

Preheat the oven to 180°C (350°F) Gas 4.

Put the chocolate pieces and butter in a heatproof bowl set over a pan of simmering water. Do not let the bottom of the bowl touch the water. Leave for several minutes until the chocolate has melted, then remove the bowl from the pan and leave to cool slightly.

Whisk together the eggs and the sugar with a handheld electric whisk. Pour in the melted chocolate mixture, then add the salt and finally the flour. Whisk until well blended. Pour the mixture into the prepared tin and bake in the centre of the preheated oven for 23–25 minutes (you have to be precise with brownies!). The outside should look crackled and the inside will feel firm to the touch but will be gooey underneath. Remove from the oven and leave to cool in the tin for 15 minutes, then slice into squares or bars.

To make the vanilla cream, take a small, sharp knife and run it carefully down the length of the vanilla pod. Open out the pod and scrape out the tiny black seeds with the tip of the knife. Stir the vanilla seeds into the crème fraîche and serve with a brownie square or two.

250 g plain chocolate, broken into pieces

250 g unsalted butter, at room temperature

4 large eggs, beaten

325 g caster sugar

½ teaspoon salt

125 g self-raising flour

25 g cocoa powder

Vanilla cream

200 g crème fraîche

1 vanilla pod

a baking tin, 20 x 30 cm, greased and lined with greaseproof paper

chocolate and *cinnamon* brownies

makes 12

V

These are sophisticated brownies, made with plain and white chocolate, so the better the chocolate, the better they will taste. Most people can't resist eating them the minute they come out of the oven. Perfect with a cup of coffee.

75 g shelled hazelnuts

275 g plain chocolate, broken into pieces

225 g unsalted butter

3 eggs

225 g caster sugar

75 g self-raising flour

2 teaspoons ground cinnamon

100 g white chocolate chips

a baking tin, 18 x 28 cm, greased and lined with greaseproof paper

Preheat the oven to 190°C (375°F) Gas 5.

Put the hazelnuts into a dry frying pan and toast over medium heat until aromatic. They burn quickly so keep an eye on them and shake the pan regularly. Leave them to cool, then chop coarsely.

Put the chocolate pieces and butter in a heatproof bowl set over a pan of simmering water. Do not let the bottom of the bowl touch the water. Leave for several minutes until the chocolate has melted, then remove the bowl from the pan and leave to cool slightly. Put the eggs and sugar into another bowl and beat until pale. Stir in the melted chocolate, flour, cinnamon, white chocolate chips and hazelnuts. Pour the mixture into the prepared tin and bake in the preheated oven for 35–40 minutes until the top sets but the mixture still feels soft underneath. Remove from the oven and leave to cool in the tin for 15 minutes, then slice into squares.

peanut butter brownies

Chocolate and peanuts are a classic combination. Use peanut butter with no added sugar or fat as it gives the best flavour.

makes
16

V

Preheat the oven to 180°C (350°F) Gas 4.

Put the chocolate pieces and butter in a heatproof bowl set over a pan of simmering water. Do not let the bottom of the bowl touch the water. Leave for several minutes until the chocolate has melted, then remove the bowl from the pan and leave to cool slightly. Break the eggs into another bowl and beat well with a handheld electric whisk. Add the sugar and whisk until the mixture is very thick and mousse-like. Whisk in the melted chocolate. Sift the flour and cocoa onto the mixture and mix until well combined. Spoon the mixture into the prepared tin.

Put all the ingredients for the peanut mixture into a bowl and mix well. Drop teaspoonfuls of the mixture, evenly spaced, onto the chocolate mixture. Use a teaspoon handle to marble or swirl both mixtures. Scatter the peanuts over the top. Bake in the preheated oven for about 30 minutes or until just firm. Remove from the oven and leave to cool in the tin for 15 minutes, then slice into squares or bars.

100 g plain chocolate, broken into pieces

175 g unsalted butter, diced

3 large eggs

200 g muscovado sugar

120 g plain flour

2 tablespoons cocoa powder

Peanut mixture

180 g smooth peanut butter

50 g caster sugar

1 tablespoon plain flour

5 tablespoons milk

2 tablespoons roasted, unsalted peanuts

a baking tin, 20.5 x 25.5 cm, greased and lined with greaseproof paper

mint brownies

125 g plain chocolate, broken into pieces

100 g unsalted butter, diced

3 large eggs

200 g caster sugar

100 g plain flour

2 tablespoons cocoa powder

100 g–200 g bittersweet chocolate with mint centre (depending on strength of flavour required)

a baking tin, 20.5 x 25.5 cm, greased and lined with greaseproof paper

makes 20

V

For this unusual brownie recipe you'll need a box (or bar) of bittersweet chocolate with a soft, mint-flavoured fondant centre, of the type that is most often sold as 'after-dinner' mints. The mints turn these brownies into a dessert fit for fine dining with friends.

Preheat the oven to 180°C (350°F) Gas 4.

Put the chocolate and butter in a heatproof bowl set over a pan of simmering water. Do not let the bottom of the bowl touch the water. Leave for several minutes until the chocolate has melted, then remove the bowl from the pan and leave to cool slightly.

Whisk the eggs with a handheld electric whisk, then add the sugar and beat until thick and mousse-like. Whisk in the melted chocolate. Sift the flour and cocoa onto the mixture and stir in. When thoroughly combined spoon half the brownie mixture into the prepared tin and spread evenly.

Leave the mint chocolates whole or break them up (depending on the size of the ones you are using). Arrange them over the brownie mixture already in the tin. Spoon the remaining brownie mixture on top and gently spread to cover the chocolate mints.

Bake in the preheated oven for about 25 minutes or until a skewer inserted halfway between the sides and the centre comes out just clean (though some of the sticky mint layer will appear). Remove from the oven and leave to cool in the tin for 15 minutes, then slice into squares or bars.

classic *flapjacks*

These flapjacks taste so good that it's hard to believe they are a healthy and sustaining snack to keep you going for hours.

Preheat the oven to 150°C (300°F) Gas 2.

Melt the butter in a large saucepan, add the syrup and sugar and stir until the sugar has dissolved. Remove from the heat and stir in the oats. Spoon the mixture into the prepared baking tin and bake in the preheated oven for 20 minutes. When done, cut into squares straightaway and leave to cool.

makes
8

V

200 g unsalted butter

1 tablespoon golden syrup

200 g soft brown sugar

250 g rolled oats

a shallow baking tin, 20 x 30 cm, lined with greaseproof paper

honeyjacks

You can use any type of honey in this recipe because they all become runny when heated.

Preheat the oven to 150°C (300°F) Gas 2.

Melt the butter in a large saucepan, add the syrup, sugar and honey, then stir until the sugar has dissolved. Remove from the heat and stir in the oats and raisins. Spoon the mixture into the prepared baking tin, sprinkle with the coconut and bake in the preheated oven for 20 minutes. When done, cut into squares straightaway and leave to cool before eating.

makes
8

V

200 g unsalted butter

1 tablespoon golden syrup

125 g soft brown sugar

75 g honey

200 g rolled oats

50 g raisins or sultanas

100 g desiccated coconut

a shallow baking tin, 20 x 30 cm, lined with greaseproof paper

nutty jacks

Nuts are high in protein and fibre, so they make a healthy addition to flapjacks. Use whichever type of nuts you like.

Preheat the oven to 150°C (300°F) Gas 2.

Melt the butter in a large saucepan, add the syrup and sugar and stir until the sugar has dissolved. Remove from the heat and stir in the oats and nuts. Spoon the mixture into the prepared baking tin and bake in the preheated oven for 20 minutes. When done, cut into squares straightaway and leave to cool. Drizzle the melted chocolate over the nutty jacks in a zigzag pattern and leave to set before eating.

makes
8

V

200 g butter

1 tablespoon golden syrup

200 g soft brown sugar

200 g rolled oats

50 g chopped nuts

100–200 g plain chocolate, melted

a shallow baking tin, 20 x 30 cm, lined with greaseproof paper

nutty *plum* crumble

serves
4

V

12 plums, halved and stoned

2–3 thick strips of zest and the juice from 1 unwaxed orange

75 g soft brown sugar

125 g unsalted butter, chilled and diced

100 g self-raising flour

50 g ground almonds

25 g flaked almonds

25 g pine nuts

cream or custard, to serve (optional)

an ovenproof dish

Pine nuts and almonds with their toasty flavours add another dimension to this crumble. They make for a biscuity, tasty crust which needs to settle before it crisps up, so leave the crumble to cool down slightly and eat it when it's warm rather than piping hot. Serve with cream or custard if you want to push the boat out. Some of the other winning fruit combinations you could try are apple and blackberry, apple and pear, or mango and banana.

Preheat the oven to 180°C (350°F) Gas 4.

Put the plums in the ovenproof dish – there should be enough room left to accommodate the crumble topping. Add the orange zest and juice. Sprinkle over 2 tablespoons of the sugar and dot over 25 g of the butter. Cover with aluminium foil and bake in the preheated oven for 25–30 minutes, or until the plums are beginning to soften.

Put the flour, ground almonds and the remaining butter in a bowl and rub until it forms small lumps. Stir in the flaked almonds, pine nuts and the remaining sugar.

Remove the dish from the oven, discard the foil and scatter over the crumble topping. Bake for 30 minutes, or until the topping is golden and the juices are bubbling through. Remove from the oven and leave to stand for 10 minutes to allow the crust to firm up. Transfer to bowls and serve with cream or custard, if you like.

nectarine and *ginger* crumble

This is a useful recipe for when nectarines are slightly hard, as cooking them softens the flesh and brings out the flavour. Ginger goes particularly well with this fruit so ginger biscuits have been used here but if they are not available, simply substitute them with any favourite crunchy biscuit and add a good pinch or two of ground ginger to the topping mixture.

serves
4

V

6 nectarines (or a mixture of peaches and plums)

2 tablespoons finely chopped fresh ginger

75 ml apple juice

50 g caster sugar

vanilla ice cream, to serve

Ginger topping

100 g unsalted butter, melted

200 g ginger nut biscuits, crushed

100 g demerera sugar

a baking tray

a shallow ovenproof dish

Preheat the oven to 190°C (375°F) Gas 5 and set the baking tray on the middle shelf to heat.

Cut the nectarines in half, twist to separate the fruit into halves, then prise out the stones. Slice or chop the flesh, tip it into the ovenproof dish and mix with the apple juice, chopped ginger and sugar.

To make the ginger topping, melt the butter in a saucepan and stir in the crushed ginger nut biscuits and sugar until the mixture resembles rough breadcrumbs. (At this stage you can pop it into a plastic bag and chill in the fridge until needed.)

Lightly sprinkle the topping mixture evenly over the surface of the nectarines, mounding it up a little towards the centre.

Place the ovenproof dish on top of the baking tray in the preheated oven and bake for about 25 minutes, until crisp and golden on top. Remove from the oven and leave to cool for 5 minutes before serving with ice cream.

500 g rhubarb, chopped

5 cm fresh ginger, peeled and finely grated

2 tablespoons caster sugar

7 bananas, peeled and thickly cut diagonally

¼ teaspoon ground cinnamon

crème fraîche or double cream, to serve

Oat topping

125 g plain flour

90 g unsalted butter, chilled and diced

125 g demerara sugar

50 g rolled oats

an ovenproof dish

rhubarb, ginger and *banana* crumble

serves **4**

V

This version of the traditional rhubarb crumble is given a banana twist, which makes a wicked combination with the ginger and crunchy oats in the crumble topping. Serve with a dollop of crème fraîche or thick cream for a winning pudding.

Preheat the oven to 200°C (400°F) Gas 6.

Put the rhubarb in a medium saucepan and add the ginger, sugar and 2 tablespoons water. Bring to the boil and simmer for 7–10 minutes, until the rhubarb has softened. Mash with a fork until you get a rough purée. Transfer to the ovenproof dish and top with the bananas and a sprinkling of cinnamon.

Put the flour and butter in a bowl and, using your fingertips, rub the butter into the flour until it looks like breadcrumbs. Add the sugar and two-thirds of the oats. Sprinkle over the fruit mixture and top with the remaining oats. Bake in the preheated oven for 30–40 minutes. Serve hot with crème fraîche.

---

100 g butter

125 g caster sugar

125 ml milk

2 eggs

1 teaspoon vanilla extract

125 g self-raising flour

60 g cocoa powder

Chocolate swamp

180 g soft brown sugar

30 g cocoa powder

250 ml boiling water

a 1-litre capacity ovenproof dish, greased

chocolate swamp pudding

serves **4**

V

Melt-in-the-mouth chocolate sponge floating in a rich chocolate sauce – this is a pudding to die for.

Preheat the oven to 180°C (350°F) Gas 4.

Put the butter, sugar and milk in a saucepan and heat gently until the sugar has dissolved. Set aside to cool.

Whisk the eggs in a bowl and add the vanilla. Sift the flour and cocoa into a large bowl, add the milk and the egg mixture and stir until smooth. Pour into the prepared dish and set aside.

To make the chocolate swamp, mix the sugar and cocoa powder together, then sprinkle evenly over the top of the pudding. Pour on the boiling water and bake in the preheated oven for 25 minutes.

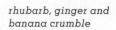

rhubarb, ginger and banana crumble

free-form caramelized peach tart

free-form *caramelized peach* tart

This is such a simple recipe – buy the pastry ready-made (choose an all-butter one for the most indulgent flavour) and shape it into a rustic-looking tart. You don't even need a tart tin!

Preheat the oven to 230°C (450°F) Gas 8.

Roll out the pastry on a lightly floured work surface and cut out a circle, 28 cm in diameter, using the plate as a template. Lift onto the baking tray and make an edge by twisting the pastry over itself all the way around the edge. Press to seal. Still on the baking tray, chill or freeze for 15 minutes.

Peel the peaches if necessary, then cut them in half, twist to separate the fruit into halves and prise out the stones. Cut the flesh into slices. Put the butter into a saucepan, then add the lemon juice and half the sugar. Heat until melted, then add the peaches and toss gently. Pile the peaches all over the pastry. Sprinkle with the remaining sugar and bake in the preheated oven for 20–25 minutes until golden, puffed and caramelized.

serves
6

V

500 g shop-bought puff pastry

4–6 ripe peaches or nectarines

55 g unsalted butter

juice of ½ a lemon

150 g caster sugar

a dinner plate, 28 cm in diameter (to use as a template)

a baking tray

quick french *apple* tart

To make this tart sensational and fit for a special occasion, make sure the apples are sliced as finely as possible and that they are arranged neatly and elegantly.

Preheat the oven to 200°C (400°F) Gas 6.

Roll out the pastry to a rectangle measuring 30 x 18 cm. Place on the baking tray and brush all over with the egg.

Cut the apples into quarters, then slice thinly and arrange in rows on top of the pastry, leaving a 5-cm gap around the edges. Drizzle the melted butter over the apples, sprinkle with sugar and dust with cinnamon. Brush the edges of the pastry with the remaining egg, then fold the edges inwards and gently press down.

Bake the tart in the preheated oven for 30 minutes. Reduce the heat to 180°C (350°F) Gas 4 and bake for another 15 minutes until the tart is golden. Serve hot or at room temperature.

serves
4

V

250 g shop-bought puff pastry

1 egg, beaten with a fork

4 red apples, cored

30 g butter, melted

2 tablespoons soft brown sugar

½ teaspoon ground cinnamon

a baking tray, lightly greased

lemon polenta cake

serves
4

V

250 g unsalted butter, diced

250 g caster sugar

4 eggs

3 unwaxed lemons

125 g polenta

125 g self-raising flour

single cream, to serve

an ovenproof dish, 20 cm in diameter, lightly greased

Polenta is Italian cornmeal that is mostly used in savoury dishes, but works well in cakes to give them a coarse texture.

Preheat the oven to 180°C (350°F) Gas 4.

Put the butter into a mixing bowl, add the sugar and beat until creamy and smooth. Beat in the eggs one at a time.

Grate the zest and squeeze the juice from 2½ of the lemons. Slice the remaining lemon half and set aside. Add the lemon zest and juice to the cake mixture and mix well. Add the polenta and flour, fold in until evenly blended, then spoon into the prepared dish. Arrange the reserved lemon slices around the middle of the cake. Bake in the preheated oven for 25 minutes. Reduce the heat to 160°C (325°F) Gas 3 and cook for 10 minutes, until a knife inserted in the centre comes out clean. Serve with cream.

devil's food cake

serves
6–8

V

100 g unsalted butter

100 g soft light brown sugar

100 g golden syrup

150 g plain flour

30 g cocoa powder

1 egg, beaten

1 teaspoon bicarbonate of soda

150 ml milk

Frosting

3 tablespoons cocoa powder

3 tablespoons hot water

100 g butter, softened

200 g icing sugar

1 tablespoon golden syrup

2 drops of vanilla extract

2 sandwich tins, 18 cm in diameter, greased

Wickedly rich and chocolatey, this cake will have everyone clamouring for more.

Preheat the oven to 180°C (350°F) Gas 4.

Put the butter, sugar and golden syrup in a saucepan and heat gently until the sugar has dissolved.

Sift the flour and cocoa into a bowl, add the butter mixture and stir well. Add the egg and mix again. Combine the bicarbonate of soda with the milk, add to the bowl and mix thoroughly. Divide the mixture between the prepared cake tins and smooth out with a palette knife. Bake in the preheated oven for 20 minutes, until just firm to the touch. Turn onto a wire rack to cool.

To make the frosting, put the cocoa in a bowl and mix in the hot water. Add the butter, sugar, golden syrup and vanilla and beat until smooth.

When the cakes are cold, sandwich together with some of the frosting. Dip a palette knife in hot water to prevent the frosting sticking to it. Spread the remainder over the top and sides of the cake.

*lemon
polenta cake*

carrot cake

A scrumptious teatime treat – no wonder it's also known as 'passion cake'!

serves
6–8

V

Preheat the oven to 180°C (350°F) Gas 4.

Put the egg yolks and sugar in a bowl and whisk until thick and creamy. Add all the remaining ingredients, except the egg white, and fold carefully until the mixture is smooth.

Whisk the egg whites until stiff, then fold into the cake mixture. Pour into the prepared tin and bake in the centre of the preheated oven for 1 hour. When done, leave the cake to cool in the tin for 5 minutes, then turn out and leave to cool completely on a wire rack.

To make the frosting, beat the cheese and icing sugar together with a wooden spoon until light and fluffy. Add a little orange zest and juice to flavour. Spread over the top of the cold cake using a palette knife dipped in hot water. Sprinkle with the remaining orange zest.

4 eggs, separated

240 g soft brown sugar

zest and juice of 1 orange

240 g ground walnuts

1 teaspoon ground cinnamon

250 g carrot, grated

100 g wholemeal flour

1 teaspoon baking powder

Frosting

200 g cream cheese

100 g icing sugar

finely grated zest and juice of 1 small orange

a loose-bottomed cake tin, 20 cm square, greased

banana cake

This cake is popular even with those who don't like bananas. The flavour improves with keeping, so wrap the cake in clingfilm and keep for a couple of days before cutting.

serves
6–8

V

Preheat the oven to 180°C (350°F) Gas 4.

Put the sugar and golden syrup in a bowl. Put the oil, eggs, bananas and vanilla in another bowl and whizz with a handheld electric whisk. Add to the bowl of sugar and mix until smooth. Fold in the flour and baking powder, then spoon into the prepared tin. Bake in the middle of the preheated oven for 50–60 minutes. When it is done, a skewer inserted in the centre of the cake should come out clean.

175 g caster sugar

1 tablespoon golden syrup

200 ml vegetable oil

2 eggs

2 ripe bananas, peeled and mashed

1 teaspoon vanilla extract

300 g self-raising flour

1 teaspoon baking powder

a 1-kg loaf tin, lightly greased

lemon drizzle loaf

175 g unsalted butter, softened

350 g caster sugar

3 large eggs, at room temperature

250 g self-raising flour

¼ teaspoon baking powder

2 unwaxed lemons

115 ml milk, at room temperature

a 900-g loaf tin, greased and lined with greaseproof paper

serves
6–8

V

Unwaxed lemons are best if you can find them, because you need both the skin and juice for this simple but tangy loaf cake.

Preheat the oven to 180°C (350°F) Gas 4.

Put the butter, 250 g of the sugar and eggs in a large bowl. Sift in the flour and baking powder. Grate the zest from the lemons straight into the bowl, then reserve the lemons.

Add the milk, then beat with a wooden spoon or handheld electric whisk (on low speed) for 1 minute until smooth and well mixed, with no streaks of flour.

Spoon the mixture into the prepared tin and bake in the preheated oven for 50–55 minutes. A skewer inserted in the centre should come out clean. If it is sticky with mixture, then bake the loaf for another 5 minutes.

While the loaf is cooking, make the drizzle. Squeeze the juice from the reserved lemons into a small bowl. Add the remaining sugar and stir for 1 minute until the sugar has dissolved and you have a syrupy glaze.

When the loaf is cooked, remove it from the oven and stand the tin on a wire cooling rack. Prick the top of the loaf all over with a cocktail stick to make small holes. Spoon the lemon syrup all over the top so it trickles into the holes. Leave until completely cold before lifting the cake out of the tin. Peel off the greaseproof paper and cut the loaf into thick slices.

apple cake

apple cake

This looks every bit as delicious as it tastes. It makes a scrumptious dessert with some ice cream, but is also good for tucking into a lunchbox or picnic hamper.

Preheat the oven to 150°C (300°F) Gas 2.

Beat the butter and sugar together in a large bowl with a handheld electric whisk until smooth, light and fluffy. Add the eggs, a little at a time, stirring well between each addition. Stir in the almonds, flour, baking powder and lemon zest, and finally the milk. Spoon the mixture into the loaf tin.

Cut the apples into thin slices. Arrange evenly over the cake. Bake in the preheated oven for 45 minutes or so, until the cake has risen and is golden and springy to the touch. Remove the cake from the oven and leave to cool in the tin for 20 minutes, then turn out onto a wire rack to cool completely. Dust with icing sugar.

serves
6–8

V

150 g butter

150 g caster sugar

2 eggs, lightly beaten
with a fork

150 g ground almonds

50 g plain flour

1 teaspoon baking powder

grated zest of
1 unwaxed lemon

100 ml milk

2 red apples, cored

icing sugar, to dust

*a 450-g loaf tin, greased
and just the base lined
with greaseproof paper*

basic cake

This light, moist sponge cake can be dressed up or down to suit any occasion. Use it as a base for your favourite flavourings.

Preheat the oven to 180°C (350°F) Gas 4.

Put the margarine and sugar in a bowl and beat with a wooden spoon until light and fluffy. Beat in the eggs, then stir in the vanilla. Sift in the flour and baking powder, then fold together quickly with a large spoon (speed at this stage keeps the cake light). Spoon the mixture into the prepared tin and bake in the middle of the preheated oven for 30–35 minutes. When done, a skewer inserted in the centre of the cake should come out clean; if it doesn't, cook for a further 5–10 minutes. Leave to cool in the tin for 5 minutes, then turn out onto a wire rack and leave to cool completely.

To make the icing, sift the sugar into a bowl and stir in the lemon juice. Carefully add a little water to make a smooth, stiff paste. Use a wet palette knife to spread the icing over the top. Leave to set before serving.

serves
6–8

V

300 g soft margarine

300 g caster sugar

5 eggs

1 teaspoon vanilla extract

350 g self-raising flour

1 teaspoon baking powder

Icing

200 g icing sugar

juice of 1 lemon

*a shallow baking tin,
20 x 30 cm, lined with
greaseproof paper*

chocolate chocolate chip cake

100 g plain chocolate, broken into pieces

100 g unsalted butter

200 g caster sugar

200 g cream cheese (not low-fat)

2 eggs

200 g plain flour

1½ teaspoons baking powder

a pinch of salt

100 g plain chocolate chips

a loaf tin, 27.5 x 8.5 cm, greased and lined with greaseproof paper

serves
6–8

V

This is a basic chocolate cake but you can either keep it simple, as in the recipe below, or add a few unbeatable additions. Try a good handful or so of mini marshmallows thrown in with the chocolate chips. Coarsely chopped almonds or hazelnuts are good as well, or instead of. If you were to add a heaped teaspoon of ground cinnamon, it would have a distinctly Mexican flavour. Despite the cream cheese, a generous dollop of something else creamy makes it even better.

Preheat the oven to 190°C (375°F) Gas 5.

Put the chocolate and butter in a heatproof bowl set over a pan of simmering water. Do not let the bottom of the bowl touch the water. Leave for several minutes until the chocolate has melted, then remove the bowl from the pan and leave to cool slightly.

Put the sugar and cream cheese in a mixing bowl and beat with a handheld electric whisk (on high speed) until well blended. Add the eggs and melted chocolate and continue beating until well mixed.

Put the flour, baking powder and salt in another bowl and mix well. Add to the cream cheese mixture, with the whisk on low speed, until just blended. Fold in the chocolate chips. Pour into the prepared tin and bake in the preheated oven for about 40–45 minutes. A skewer inserted in the centre should come out clean.

index

recipe credits

Nadia Arumugam
Indonesian fried rice
Sweet and sour pork

Susannah Blake
Giant prosciutto, brie and
  tomato toasts
Mushrooms on toast
Nutty chocolate and
  marshmallow toast
Spicy fried potatoes and
  chorizo on toast
Tomato, basil and mozzarella
  toasts
Tuna melt

Tamsin Burnett-Hall
Bean burritos
Chickpea and vegetable
  bulghur pilau
Moussaka-filled aubergines
Tarragon chicken casserole

Maxine Clark
Sausage and bacon rolls
Muffin mania
Butternut squash, sage and
  chilli risotto
Parmesan and butter risotto
Quiche Lorraine
Sausage, sun-dried tomato
  and potato tart
Free-form caramelized peach
  tart
Creamy tomato and bread
  soup
Grilled portobello mushrooms
Roast peppers stuffed with
  pasta
Nectarine and ginger crumble

Linda Collister
Bang bang chicken
Beef rendang
Cinnamon toast
Double chocolate muffins
Guacamole
Home-baked tortilla chips
Italian roast chicken
Lemon drizzle loaf
Mint brownies
Pea and Parmesan risotto
Peanut butter brownies
Roasties
Toad-in-the-hole

Ross Dobson
Asparagus tagliatelle
Baked pasta with aubergine...
Chunky chickpea soup
Courgette and tomato risotto
Garlic and chilli rice soup
Miso soup with ramen noodles
Scotch broth
Sesame chicken and
  vegetable noodle salad

Silvana Franco
Creamy smoked salmon pasta
English breakfast pizza
Lasagne
Margherita pizza
Pasta and bean soup
Pasta with Parma ham...
Pasta with puttanesca sauce
Pasta with roasted aubergine...
Penne with broccoli...
Pepperoni pizza
Quattro stagioni pizza
Roasted pepper pizza
Soup with pasta shells, peas...
Spaghetti Bolognese
Summer minestrone
Three-cheese baked penne
White spaghetti

Liz Franklin
Apple cake
Cannellini beans with garlic...
Lemony poached chicken
Little fried mozzarella and
  tomato sandwiches
Meatloaf
Pea, sausage and onion
  calzone
Rosemary potatoes
Super-easy lamb skewers

Tonia George
Chicken avgolemono
Chickpea, tomato and chorizo
  soup
Chocolate brownies
Courgette, broad bean and
  lemon broth
Couscous with feta, dill...
Cumin-spiced lamb cutlets
Minty pea risotto soup
Nutty plum crumble
Puy lentil and vegetable soup
Rigatoni with pork...
Split pea and sausage soup
Steak with new potatoes,
  Roquefort and rocket
Sweetcorn and pancetta
  chowder

Brian Glover
Fish baked with lemon,
  oregano and potatoes

Nicola Graimes
Bubble and squeak patties
Mozzarella and tuna
  quesadilla
Pesto and mozzarella toastie
Sardines and tomato on toast
Vegetable, ham and barley
  broth
Turkey and bay skewers
Pork with sweet potato mash
Rigatoni with bacon...
Grilled peaches

Rachael Anne Hill
Baked sweet potatoes
Broccoli cheese
Cheat's cherry brûlée
Cheat's mini pizzas
Flaked haddock moussaka
Foil-baked salmon
Leeks and tomatoes on toast
Tuna pasta salad
Tuscan tuna and bean pasta

Jennifer Joyce
Bacon, potato and Red
  Leicester panini
Gruyère, mature Cheddar
  and spring onion panini

Caroline Marson
Beef fajitas
Moroccan-style roasted
  vegetable couscous
Pepperoni, red pepper and
  crouton frittata
Roast chicken with garlic...
Stir-fried seafood

Jane Noraika
Rhubarb, ginger and banana
  crumble
Roasted vegetable dauphinois
Sesame sweet potato wedges

Elsa Petersen-Schepelern
Minestrone

Louise Pickford
Cheese on toast
Cherry tomato puttanesca
  sauce
Chicken lemon skewers
Chocolate and cinnamon
  brownies
Fusilli with sausage ragu
Greek country salad
Lamb in pita bread
Prawn fried rice
Roasted tomato sauce
Soured cream coleslaw
Stir-fried sesame cabbage
Tomato, caper and anchovy
  pizza

Jennie Shapter
Baked brunch omelette
Chilli chicken enchiladas
Minted courgette frittata
Onion and blue cheese
  omelette
Spaghetti and rocket frittata

Fiona Smith
Garlic and tomato naan
Greek barley salad
New potato, crisp salami and
  sesame salad
Roast potatoes, chorizo and
  lemon
Tzatziki

Sunil Vijayakar
Chicken and spinach curry
Mince and pea curry
Spiced aubergine dhal

Fran Warde
Banana cake
Basic cake
Beefburgers
Carrot cake
Chocolate swamp pudding
Classic flapjacks
Creamy mustard mash
Devil's food cake
Farmhouse sauté
Fish cakes
French pancakes
French toast and fried
  tomatoes
Garlic and parsley bread
Honeyjacks
Indian lamb curry
Lemon polenta cake
Noodle mountain
Nutty jacks
Parma ham-wrapped salmon
Plum clafoutis
Potato skins with green dip

Laura Washburn
Baked amaretti peaches
Chicken with tomato, garlic...
Chocolate chocolate chip cake
Kitchen garden soup
Pasta with ricotta...
Potato wedges
Vodka risotto

Lindy Wildsmith
Carbonara
Spaghetti with garlic...
Tuna, coriander and lemon
  pasta with tomato salad

Potatoes boulangère
Prawn curry
Quick French apple tart
Ratatouille
Rice noodle salad with prawns
Risotto primavera
Scrambled eggs
Spicy vegetable wrap
Thai green chicken curry
Three-cheese cauliflower
Toasted oat yoghurt
Vegetable noodle stir-fry
Vegetable, seed and nut cakes

photography credits

Key: a=above, b=below, r=right, l=left, c=centre.

Caroline Arber
Pages 17a, 36r, 37, 52, 75, 76,
96, 185, 197a, 201, 216, 228

Martin Brigdale
Pages 55, 107b, 112, 131, 132,
149a, 149c, 172, 175, 189, 224

Peter Cassidy
Pages 3 all, 6, 8, 11 all, 12bl,
12-13a, 13a, 13b, 23l, 57a, 57b,
80, 84, 87, 91, 92, 106, 107c, 115,
127, 136, 182, 190, 212, 220

Vanessa Davies
Pages 18, 99, 103l, 107a, 128,
178r, 186, 194, 205, 231

Nicki Dowey
Pages 4-5, 28, 95, 121l, 159r, 206

Dan Duchars
Page 196

Tara Fisher
Pages 17c, 38, 144, 164, 168

Lisa Linder
Pages 31, 47, 103r, 232

William Lingwood
Pages 23r, 24, 27, 36l, 44, 66,
69, 79, 88, 108, 121r, 122, 147,

154, 159l, 193, 198, 223

Richard Jung
Pages 58, 61, 119, 149b, 150,
153, 160, 167, 171, 197c, 213, 215

Diana Miller
Pages 21, 100, 140

David Munns
Pages 14ar, 17b, 43r, 125l, 163,
235

Noel Murphy
Pages 41, 43l, 51, 70r, 202

William Reavell
Pages 32, 35 both, 57c, 62, 72,
83, 104, 111, 116, 135, 139, 143,
157, 176, 181, 197b, 209, 210, 219

Yuki Sugiura
Page 65

Debi Treloar
Pages 2, 12-13a, 14al, 14bl,
15,16, 48, 56, 148, 227

Ian Wallace
Pages 1, 70l, 125r

Kate Whitaker
Page 178l

the *Student* cookbook

GREAT GRUB FOR THE HUNGRY AND THE BROKE

RYLAND

PETERS

& SMALL

LONDON NEW YORK

Senior Designer Toni Kay

Senior Editor Céline Hughes

Picture Research Emily Westlake

Production Controller Toby Marshall

Art Director Leslie Harrington

Publishing Director Alison Starling

Indexer Sandra Shotter

First published in the UK in 2009
by Ryland Peters & Small
20–21 Jockey's Fields
London WC1R 4BW
www.rylandpeters.com

10 9 8 7 6 5 4 3 2

Text © Nadia Arumugam, Susannah Blake,
Tamsin Burnett-Hall, Maxine Clark, Linda Collister, Ross
Dobson, Liz Franklin, Tonia George, Brian Glover, Nicola
Graimes, Rachael Anne Hill, Jennifer Joyce, Caroline Marson,
Jane Noraika, Louise Pickford, Jennie Shapter, Fiona Smith,
Sunil Vijayakar, Fran Warde, Laura Washburn, Lindy
Wildsmith, and Ryland Peters & Small 2009

Design and photographs © Ryland Peters & Small 2009

ISBN: 978-1-84597-884-6

The recipes in this book have been published previously
by Ryland Peters & Small.

The authors' moral rights have been asserted. All rights
reserved. No part of this publication may be reproduced,
stored in a retrieval system or transmitted in any form or
by any means, electronic, mechanical, photocopying or
otherwise, without the prior permission of the publisher.

Printed and bound in China

A CIP record for this book is available from
the British Library.

Notes:
• All spoon measurements are level, unless
otherwise specified.

• Ovens should be preheated to the specified
temperature. Recipes in this book were tested using
a regular oven. If using a fan-assisted oven, follow
the manufacturer's instructions for adjusting
temperatures.

• All eggs are medium, unless otherwise specified.
Recipes containing raw or partially cooked egg,
or raw fish or shellfish, should not be served to the
very young, very old, anyone with a compromised
immune system or pregnant women.